When Customers Talk

*...Turn What
They Tell You into Sales*

OTHER BOOKS BY T. SCOTT GROSS

Positively Outrageous Service, Second Edition

Why Service Stinks . . . and Exactly What to Do About It!

Borrowed Dreams: The Roughest, Toughest Jobs on the Planet and What I Learned from Working Them

When Customers Talk

...Turn What They Tell You into Sales

T. Scott Gross & BIGresearch

A **Kaplan Professional** Company

Vice President and Publisher: Cynthia A. Zigmund
Acquisitions Editor: Jonathan Malysiak
Senior Managing Editor: Jack Kiburz
Interior Design: Lucy Jenkins
Cover Design: Scott Rattray, Rattray Design
Typesetting: Elizabeth Pitts

Published by Dearborn Trade Publishing
A Kaplan Professional Company

Library of Congress Cataloging-in-Publication Data

Gross, T. Scott.
   When customers talk : —turn what they tell you into sales / T. Scott Gross and BIGresearch.
      p.   cm.
   Includes index.
   ISBN 0-7931-9519-5 (6 × 9 paperback)
1. Customer relations. 2. Customer services.   I. BIGresearch (Firm)   II. Title.
   HF5415.5.G762   2005
   658.8'12—dc22

                        2004023138

DEDICATION

City Slickers is a favorite movie of mine. In one memorable scene, Billy Crystal is complaining to tough-skinned trail boss Curly that life seems to be one crisis after another. Curly turns slowly in the saddle, points a gloved finger skyward, and puts life into sharp perspective.

Curly says life's distractions ". . . don't mean nothing if you know the 'one thing' that gives life meaning."

Curly would be proud of me. I've found my 'one thing.' She makes me smile and makes me more. She is the perfect partner. Her name is Melanie, but you can call her Buns. It is to Buns that I dedicate this and everything I do.

PRAISE FOR *WHEN CUSTOMERS TALK*

"I never met a successful marketer who did not have the ability to see things before they happened. If you were not born with this ability, you NEED to read this book."

> Robert Barocci, president and CEO,
> Advertising Research Foundation (ARF)

"Scott Gross, with some big-time help from his BIGresearch friends, tells us how to laser through the congestion to find out what the consumer is going to do today and tomorrow, not what they did yesterday. . . . When the customer talks, Scott listens through BIGresearch, and then gives us the future. A brilliant and fun read."

> Robin Lewis, president, Robin Reports

"BIGresearch gives us reliable and projectable insight . . . [and] with insight, we can generate more effective marketing plans. . . . BIGresearch data helps us listen to our shoppers talk. . . ."

> Ken Barnett, COO, MARS Advertising Group

"Gary Drenik, Phil Rist, and Joe Pilotta [of BIGresearch] share their understanding and insights in *When Customers Talk* in a crisp, cogent, and compelling fashion."

> Robert "Kam" Kamerschen, retired CEO, current outside director of six public companies, and a private investor

C o n t e n t s

If you could predict the future, would you do it? If you could know what your customer would want to buy tomorrow or next month or even next year, what would you do with that information?

Well, you *can* know the future, and you can use the information for better or worse. It is up to you. But if you fail to listen and learn, don't blame us, because we're about to show you how you can get to the buying decision before your customer has even left the house!

Once we show you where the customer is going, we'll backtrack, only slightly, and show you where (or why) the customer is leaving. Take, for example, auto sales. Customers have been leaving U.S. auto brands for years, and the automakers still haven't a clue.

As this book is being written, the major U.S. automakers have reported a profitable quarter, their first in a very long time. How did they do it? They did it by instituting some of the most generous incentive programs in the history of car sales. Did they have the product customers really wanted? No. To move their product, they had to bribe customers into purchasing inventory, which was at record high levels (100 days of vehicle inventory as opposed to the preferable 30 to 60).

We could have told them a year ago that their customers were leaving (you probably could have done the same), and that tastes in product weren't changing—had *already* changed. The Big Three just didn't see it. They hadn't looked into the future, but they could have. They didn't see where the customer was going. That's no surprise. They haven't fully seen why the customer is leaving.

And for what reason is the customer leaving? Car salesmen!

It's a good thing shoppers don't routinely carry sidearms. If they did, it would be a bad day for car salesmen. It turns out that consumers hate them, don't trust them, and generally think the world would be a better place without them!

We asked 100,000 very vocal consumers to help us write this book. We asked, and boy, did they ever talk! The response had all the subtlety of drinking from a fire hose. We questioned gently, and they shouted back their response.

Consumers are angry. They are fed up, sick and tired, and looking for an excuse to fight (or switch). They're not impressed with the quality of products, and they think service is awful and trending worse. If you are a retailer, the things they told us would curl your hair!

We listened via the Internet. Our analysis was via computer and special software that until recently was a government secret. While not exactly the same, our software is at least similar to the software created to monitor Web traffic in the war against terrorism. Not only do we have plenty of data, we can cut it in a near-infinite number of ways.

And we're going to do just that. As the pages turn, we'll clue you in on what to do to anticipate your customer's next move. We'll tell you what you must do to attract and retain profitable customers, and give you ideas about what you must do tomorrow. And we'll show you how to use your knowledge about customers to effectively beat your competition.

We won't shackle you to a static book. Instead, we'll invite you to a Web site specially designed with retailers in mind. And you're going to love it. We should know. After all, we can see the future—yours and ours!

A LITTLE BIT ABOUT BIGRESEARCH

Each month for nearly four years, BIGresearch invited nearly 10,000 online panelists to share their opinions, reveal their shopping habits, and describe their buying, saving, and investing intentions. This book was really written by that panel of very vocal consumers.

But before there was a panel and set of survey questions, there was an idea, and that idea—a really BIG idea—was the brainchild of three very smart guys: Phil Rist, Gary Drenik, and Joe Pilotta. Rist, Drenik, and Pilotta wear degrees, awards, and articles in prestigious journals like Mr. T wore gold chains. (Since meeting this trio, I no longer consider myself a geek.)

It's not that they are boring; I think they just live in a slightly different dimension. They are fun guys, in their own inimitable way. I just don't always get what they are saying, so I have been reduced to laughing whether or not I really got the point. I figure these guys are so smart, if they said it and laughed, the only reasonable thing to do was laugh with them!

When we first struck our partnership, I had the idea that I would be the writer. Wrong. They didn't send material for the book; they just sent data—and lots of it. CDs full of it. That's when I realized that this project would be less about writing and a whole lot about interpreting. The very idea of predictive surveying, I find, is incredibly interesting. It is an elegantly simple idea whose time has come. My job was to make the concept accessible, useful, and interesting to the average business reader.

To be at least a little bit serious, Phil, Gary, Joe, and the entire staff of BIGresearch have been a pleasure to work with, and even though the project has reached a major milestone with the publishing of *When Customers Talk,* I'm sticking around. After all, the boys tell me they may need more of that "folksy stuff," and besides, I'm beginning to understand them on the first pass.

—T. Scott Gross

1

WE SEE TOMORROW

It was 1955. The old Plymouth rattled along 41st Street, the exhaust fumes choking kids playing in the street as it passed. The Plymouth was used-to-be green, a color brought by years of driving long Ohio winters in the days when Ziebart was the only protection an already old automobile might have.

If we were in the Plymouth and the windows were rolled down, chances are we were heading to the wholesale bait yard north of Cincinnati, and chances are we'd be stopping at the Dairy Queen on the way home to Covington, Kentucky, across the brown Ohio River. I'd get a chocolate dip cone, my grandmother a peanut butter shake, and my grandfather (I called him Boom) would likely excuse himself to the bar next door to drink a quick five-cent Hudepohl beer.

While we waited in the car for Boom and the first cool relief brought by ice cream and a summer evening, Gran would slurp the last of her shake and lead off the entertainment, saying "Riddly, riddly, i-dee-dee; I see something that you don't see; And the color of it is . . . " And it would be red or orange or blue, because these were the days before sea mist, fawn, and ochre.

Gran could see things that I could not, even after she pointed them out. It wasn't that she had better eyes; it was that she knew how to look. (Wasn't it Yogi Berra who said, "You can see a lot by looking"?)

Pretend for a moment that your desk is a '47 Plymouth with a shift lever on the column and vacuum-operated wipers. It's no longer 1955; it's tomorrow and you are at the Dairy Queen, sitting with Gran and me. Order whatever you want. And imagine that I am your boss or your shareholders or, worse, your competitors, and we are looking through the windshield and seeing the marketplace as Gran slurps the last of that peanut butter shake through a paper straw and begins the game, saying "Riddly, riddly, I-dee-dee . . ."

And what if Gran *could* see the future, and you saw only the neon glow of Struvie's Silverleaf Café?

Sit up straight. I'm going to show you something really cool! You would recognize the name of the retailer involved in a heartbeat, but, since many BIG clients recognize the competitive advantage they receive through online surveying, they, well, just don't want to talk about it out loud.

The gist of the story is this: The ad agency for our mystery retailer presented a new commercial targeted to a very niche market. After viewing the first cut, the corporate marketing folks had a hunch that they might have missed the target. But the producer was a big-time heavy hitter who promised that the 30-second ad would be an instant hit. Besides, "Our buy is for next week, and we can't lose our place. We can test it for awareness after it runs and we'll see." *After* it runs? But what if we're wrong?

The ad had one feature that the producer said would guarantee awareness, but it was that same feature—an irritating sound effect—that made the corporate guys wince, not smile, every time they played the tape. So, Wednesday morning, they plopped the tape squarely into the in-basket at BIGresearch, saying, "Help!"

The BIG folks played the tape and winced as well. But, not to worry. Late that same evening, BIG was online with a full 2,500 individuals of the exact same target audience that the commercial was supposed to woo. By Friday, the client had an answer: Yep, that sound effect irritated nearly everyone except big-time, heavy-hitter producers. And yep, it was not likely to motivate the audience to buy.

No worry. A simple edit removed the sound effect and, once again, online-based consumer research saved the day. Attempting to survey via focus group could have taken weeks, if not months. Online consumer research turned a matter of months into a matter of hours.

ABOUT THIS DATA

When confronted with data one scrap at a time, it can be hard to interpret. You can't be certain that the sample is statistically significant. But when BIGresearch dumps data onto your desk, it doesn't take long for the big picture to form.

What I have always believed, and now know for certain, is this: There is no such thing as a chain store. Every store has its own personality that is the aggregate sum of the personalities who work and shop there.

Customer service is not a matter of the logo shining atop the pole sign. Service happens on the inside, and everyone is a player. Customers influence their own service by the way they behave, and the stores they choose to shop. Bosses, by the way they hire and the way they lead, have major impact on service quality.

Institutional ads may bring customers through the door, once. It is service that brings them back.

You simply cannot separate customer service, merchandising, and marketing. When you include management and maintenance, they all work together to create this thing called a brand. And if you have read our earlier books, you know that brands are extremely local in nature.

There are no chain stores in the sense that everything is the same. For every customer who said she couldn't live without Wal-Mart, we found one that thinks Wal-Mart is the Devil Incarnate. For everyone who praises Best Buy for its wide selection and helpful service, we can find someone who thinks they are just plain awful.

When you read a comment in this book, ignore both the praise and condemnation, because every store, even in a chain, is different. And every customer and every employee are different. It is the sum of our experiences while shopping that determines whether or not we will return. A poor impression can simply mean that you were served by the wrong person on the wrong day at a time when inventory was low or a price was mismarked.

The same is true for great experiences. It's entirely possible that you got lucky.

What is terrifying to retailers is how long poor impressions can persist. Recently, Buns and I drove past a small restaurant where we had experienced poor service. "I never did like that place. Do you remember the last time we ate there?"

"Do you know it's been nearly ten years?"

In ten years, you know the help has turned at least 30 times. You know they have new management and new menu items. But it is ten years after a single bad experience, and we are pointing the nose of the SUV toward another driveway down the street.

So when you read a comment in this book that this store is fabulous or that store is the pits . . . ignore it. Better yet, just keep in mind that we are sharing one customer's point of view. Where the real value lies is in the big picture. Think how the comments may relate to you and your business, and you will take away real value.

You don't have to work for a big retailer to benefit from our studies. All you need is a passion for your business and a love for your customers. In fact, if your business is a mom-and-pop operation, all the better for you, because you have the good fortune of being naturally physically close to your customers. You can literally reach out and take the pulse of your business.

The one obstacle that big business faces is what I call the "dis-economy of scale." In personal terms, I discovered the dis-economy of scale while serving as a member of our local school board. On an average year, our local high school graduates about 30 seniors and yes, that's 100 percent of the class.

If you are a Center Point Pirate and want to play in the band, someone will find you an instrument and you're in. Do you want to play football? No problem. Coach Kaiser will find a spot for you at the field house. But what if you want to play both trumpet and tackle? Well, that's not a problem either! At halftime, you'll find your trumpet waiting at the sidelines. You can march in the halftime show and still make the locker room in time to catch the strategy for the second half.

When schools or businesses are small, there is plenty of opportunity for knowing the customer. At Center Point, no child gets lost in the shuffle. There are only 536 students from pre-K to high school senior. They're all on the same campus, and it's literally possible to put your arms around any and all of them. Your teacher knows your mom and dad. The school board president is likely to be your Sunday school teacher.

One of our seniors decided that tires are for playing with, and he did what all of us do at one time or another—he peeled out in front of the school. One of our board members witnessed this rite of passage and mentioned it to the kid's dad, saying, "I noticed your son is studying to be a stunt driver." By the time the kiddo showed up for supper, dad was waiting. That can happen in a small community.

In small systems, there is no anonymity.

FIGURE 1.1 *Little Things Can Mean a Lot When Customers Talk*

Which type of vehicle are you considering?
Consumers Planning to Buy a Vehicle in the Next 6 Months

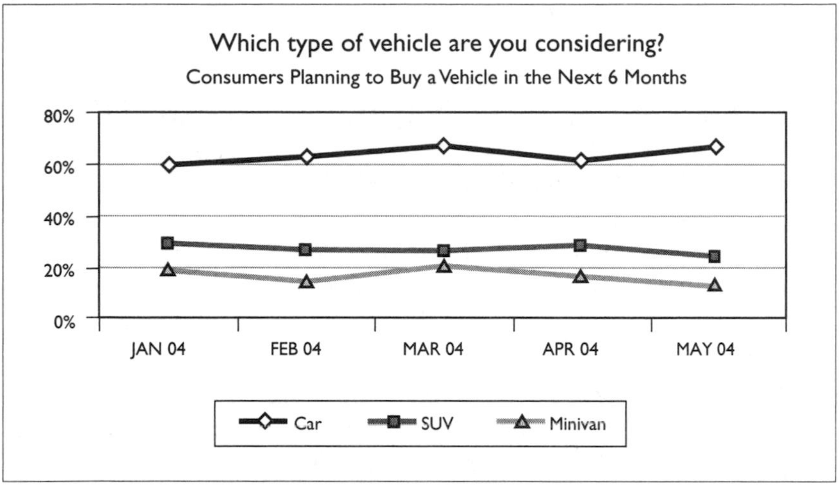

Source: BIGresearch, Consumer Intentions and Actions, May 2004.

Where big business is at a distinct disadvantage is the ease with which one can become anonymous—a customer who doesn't know the clerk, who maybe doesn't really know the manager, who quite possibly is only on greeting terms with the big boss, if that.

This book is about denying anonymity. It's about helping the management of even megachains get a little closer to the customer and be just a little more like ma and pa.

LITTLE THINGS MEAN A LOT

The differences appear subtle, but their impact can be huge.

For example, take the shift of 3.3 percent in U.S. auto sales from May to June of 2004. Three points, 3 percent, no big deal, right? Wrong. It was the difference between $63.2 billion and $61.1 billion, and now we're talking in excess of $2 billion!

If we assume that the average vehicle costs in the neighborhood of $25,000, we're looking at about 85,000 new cars or trucks that did not get built, that were not sold, that did not result in a commission. As one U.S. senator was famous for saying, "A million here, a million there, and pretty soon you're talking real money."

So read the chart in Figure 1.1 with the understanding that "little" things mean real money. Unless you ask, you will not know. But hearing is not understanding—until you recognize that even little things mean a lot when customers talk.

Understanding will only come when you recognize that even little things mean a lot when customers talk.

ACME—A CONFIDENTIAL CONVERSATION

We polished off a quick lunch at Sporty's, loved on a few customers, and headed south along the main drag of Kerrville, Texas. We had two stops to make, the first at a local, independently owned tire store, whose owner stopped earlier at Sporty's to deliver a couple of racing tires to use as a wine rack. We also suggested discussing an idea or two for co-promotion.

We parked in the first available space and didn't bother locking our car for two reasons: Kerrville is a small, friendly town, and we knew we wouldn't be long. We had one more stop to make and just enough time to conduct our business and hurry back to the office for a two o'clock phone call. To make this easy, we'll call the company Acme and my inside source, Anne, the director of research and planning.

When I pushed through the door, the rush of air-conditioning felt good, but it was the conversation at the counter that caught my attention. Wouldn't you know that two of the countermen and a local good ole boy were discussing big box discounters and their unfortunate impact on small communities and even smaller businesses. I waited my turn to jump in the debate, amused to know that in a matter of minutes I would be interviewing a representative of the devil incarnate.

Acme and the other big box discounters get blamed for everything. A small business bites the dust and who ya gonna blame? Wal-Mart. Best Buy. Borders.

"People around here will do whatever it takes to support a local business," said the lanky frame wearing cowboy boots and holding up my side of the counter.

"Ya think so?" I baited the hook.

"I know so," Tex replied with a drawl that announced his birthplace.

"Well, I can prove otherwise. One, I've seen a bit of research that says as long as the price is low and the quality is sufficient, the majority of Americans don't care where something they want or need is made or sold. And two, all you have to do is drive to San Antonio, and you'll see half of your neighbors shopping at Sam's Club."

"He's got a point," the chubby counterman rang into the conversation. "I've seen them myself."

I couldn't wait to hear from Acme.

Shortly, when the phone rang, it was my deep-cover source. The big boys are so afraid that the competition will discover the benefits of listening to customers that they rarely grant interviews. (If this were *60 Minutes,* all you would be seeing is a silhouette, and the voice would be electronically altered.) With near-military precision, my source was calling right on time, straight from the devil's den.

OK, I'm just being dramatic. Anne, and by extension the company she worked for, was on the line willing to share all but the most secret of secrets. And if you are wise, you will listen carefully and follow their lead.

Acme was an early adopter of what Anne referred to as online panels. Prior to online paneling, the bulk of Acme's paneling was done the old-fashioned way, one at a time via telephone. Did the old way work? Obviously. You don't grow a company as large as Acme by luck and guts alone. But, as Anne says, "Online paneling is better, faster, and cheaper." She then appends the remark by saying that the data comes in larger quantity and is much more flexible.

By using online panels, the responses can be "cut" by geography, income, purchase size . . . the options are limited only by your imagination. And all of this comes in a matter of days rather than months.

How significant is it to Acme's decision-making processes? "Very significant . . . because it is faster, we can integrate the voice of the customer into decisions in [near] real time . . . [and] if you say you can get feedback in a week, more people ask for insight before making a decision."

I remember reading somewhere that an estimated 25 percent of American small business owners are Acme customers. And if you consider Acme and its competition, no doubt that number is right at 100 percent. Think about it. The folks who often complain the loudest about big box discounters (particularly Costco, Sam's Club, or Staples) depend on them to help keep their costs down!

So it should be of no surprise that small business owners are prized members of Acme's online panel. The big box discounters know their customer base and naturally want to seed their online panels with folks who buy just like them. Anne and her cohorts want a large sample size, something much easier to obtain online.

The big concern is keeping the panel interested and motivated in order to keep the information flowing. With this much larger sample size, Anne oversimplifies slightly saying, "We just get more answers." And, in any research, more answers usually lead to greater insight.

I asked Anne what was the most significant action Acme had taken based on online paneling, and for a moment she seemed to be stumped.

My first thought was, "Oh, no! They just use this as a research geek's toy." And then her answers began to flow too fast for me to capture.

"We've done studies and made decisions in terms of our customer base . . . types of services, merchandising decisions, purchase intentions information . . . which categories will be hot or down . . . we find complaints or problems . . . we even get competitive info (on pricing, etc.)."

As to the future of online paneling, Anne seems to think that executives will soon begin to change their level of expectations for bringing the "voice of the consumer" directly into the decision-making process. No doubt, once online paneling is widespread and researchers learn how to keep a panel interested and motivated, the impact of the volume, speed, and flexibility of the data will be overwhelming. All this comes from a company that is legendary for its ability to mine data from its point-of-sale (POS) system.

"The difference," says Anne, "is that while the transaction data can tell a great deal about who is doing the buying, it provides only vague hints about why they buy." And a POS system yields no data at all about performance relative to the competition.

"How can your customers use online paneling to become better merchants?" This was like asking the champ where to find his soft spot.

"That's a great question! I can see small businesses participating through their [trade] associations . . . on a peer-to-peer basis by invitation only and sharing best practices. That would be a very powerful use of the medium."

I saved the best question for last in the hope of getting one of the toughest of competitors to show us the way to beat it at its own game: "How can a small business use consumer research to gain a competitive advantage over the big guys?"

There was that hesitation again, and then the voice began to explain without revealing, "We do a lot of things to understand our pricing . . . panels help us understand the perception of pricing . . . there are quantitative facts, but there are also perceptions relative to the brand, the price, the quality . . . the value proposition. We work hard to keep prices low . . . we have to know [that] our target market perceives us to have price/value leadership." Again she mentioned the value of flexible data, data that can be cut to reveal such nuances as part of the country, kind of consumer, and so on.

And that, my friends, is how the big boys say you can beat them. Simply walk around the counter, stick out your hand, and introduce yourself to the customer.

It's funny what you can learn when customers talk!

2

FOREKNOWLEDGE

"The trouble with our times is that the future is not what it used to be."
PAUL VALERY

Of all the benefits of listening to the customer, seeing the future is the most valuable. The Greeks used to consult the fabled Oracle of Delphi for a look into the future. Today, savvy trainers and marketing folks sometimes employ what is known as the Delphi Method for a quick peek into the collective thinking of small groups. BIGresearch takes the Delphi Method a step further and looks at larger groups and covers more issues, all due to the Internet and the pervasiveness of the personal computer.

The benefit of seeing into the future, even if the insight is but a matter of weeks, is that responsive organizations can make changes sufficient to modify what is no longer a foregone conclusion. The secret is twofold: First, you must be willing to look; second, you must be willing and able to react.

Let's say that the survey indicates consumers are going to delay the purchase of major appliances. If you were in the appliance business, what would you do? Or what if the survey indicated that consumers were going to pay off credit cards in greater numbers over the next few months? What would you do?

Would you make changes in a sale you had been planning? Would you adjust your product mix? What would you do? As difficult as that question may be to answer, imagine the alternative. Stumbling in the dark! BIGresearch uses two tools: one is appropriately named the CIA, and the other is the soon-to-be-famous Clusterizer.

ACQUIRING FOREKNOWLEDGE

The CIA, also known as Consumer Intentions and Actions,™ is unique in several aspects. First, it is an online survey. Surprisingly, while there are many surveys done online, there are very few marketing studies done via the Internet. Second, the survey polls approximately 10,000 potential respondents each month and regularly receives over 8,000 usable responses.

The CIA is unique in two additional ways. Because key elements of the survey are repeated month after month, the survey results reveal trends. The vast majority of surveys are little more than snapshots of consumer thinking. Surveying done the old-fashioned way produces little more than an historical document. Mail-in surveys are especially slow, and telephone surveying has all but disappeared, thanks to new regulations and the advent of caller ID. The Internet is fast, accurate, and cost-effective.

The real beauty of the CIA is that it offers a look into the future. Like traditional surveys, the CIA asks for opinions and feelings about current events. But unlike traditional surveys, the CIA asks consumers what they intend to do in the future, and it is amazingly accurate in part because of the enormous size of audience.

Some traditional survey providers say that in a country of nearly 300 million, a survey of 600 to 800 is statistically significant. CIA involves a population more than ten times larger. Rather than generating results in the typical +/– 3 to 5 percent range, the CIA is dead on at +/– 1 percent!

If you are old enough, you will remember Mr. Peabody, an erudite, eye-glass-wearing hound with a sophisticated accent and a pet boy named Sherman. They usually appeared on Saturday mornings surrounded by the adventures of Rocky and Bullwinkle. Sherman would usually kick off the episode by asking Peabody a question, the answer to which always involved a trip through time made possible by the use of the fabulous Wayback Machine.

Mr. Peabody and Sherman traveled to the past to make history turn out right. Using the CIA or something like it, we can visit the present to make the future turn out more to our favor.

FIGURE 2.1 *Home Improvement/Hardware Store Shopped Most Often*

	Feb. 2002	Feb. 2003	Equity Index
Ace Hardware	3.2%	2.9%	91.1
Home Depot	38.0%	37.9%	99.7
Lowe's	18.9%	21.2%	112.0
Sears	2.3%	1.9%	84.2
TrueValue	1.2%	1.0%	80.1

Source: BIGresearch.

Mr. Peabody's Improbable History always ended with an atrocious pun, but we will resist the temptation.

Just as an example of how the present can predict the future, our Consumer Intentions and Actions survey asked consumers if they intended to spend more, less, or the same on consumer electronics in the next 90 days. This was a question we thought surely would bring bad news, since consumers had already told us that, overall, they expected to spend less, and we had begun to see a trend toward lower traffic counts.

But 35 percent of the consumers planning to spend more on home electronics also told us that for home electronics they shop Best Buy most often. This became a solid positive for Best Buy.

If you were a manufacturer or an investor, how valuable would this knowledge be to you?

In February of 2003, the Wayforward Machine told us that there was a 12 percent increase in the number of consumers calling Lowe's their favorite DIY (do-it-yourself) center, while Home Depot remained flat and Sears actually lost share of customers. (See Figure 2.1.)

The Wayforward Machine does an incredible job at predicting the retail future. Consumers really will tell you what they want, if you know what to ask and if you actually pose the questions. They'll tell you what they are going to do tomorrow. And while any individual response may be way off the mark, collectively they will be right on the money.

The holiday season for 2002 was said to be nearly impossible to predict, since it so closely followed 9/11. Deloitte and Touche took a shot and predicted a rosy 5.5 percent bump. Ernst & Young tossed in a respectable 4.8 percent. We did the obvious—we asked consumers what they intended to spend, and they told us.

"A miserly 2.6 percent," they said, and then turned right around and proved themselves nearly right by spending 2.2 percent! If you were ordering merchandise for the holiday season, wouldn't you have loved to know this in advance?

How does the Wayforward Machine really work? Perhaps the Oracle of Delphi knew something about ants. Douglas Hofstadter wrote in *Godel, Escher, Bach* (Vintage Books, 1980) about the uncanny ability of decidedly small-brained ants to make surprisingly complex decisions. Since no one has yet to discover the existence of an ant mastermind, there has to be something else at work, something that I think explains the accuracy of the CIA survey.

Talking about the ability of ants to work together, two of Hofstadter's characters muse, "Where does the ability to converse come from? It must reside somewhere inside the colony . . . it seems to me that the situation is not unlike a human brain out of neurons. Certainly no one would insist that human being cells have to be intelligent on their own . . . even though ants as individuals wander about in what seems a random way, there are nevertheless overall trends, involving large numbers of ants, which can emerge from that chaos."

Or chalk it up to group parallel computing and call it a day.

The Clusterizer helps us interpret responses from the CIA, which in addition to traditional forced-choice responses calls for verbatim comments. How do you interpret the multiple, free-style comments of more than 8,000 respondents? You "clusterize" them!

The Clusterizer uses language-sensitive programming to group and rank comments into clusters that can in turn be grouped and ranked to create a picture of what the survey population is thinking and feeling. Is it 100 percent accurate? Not when taken one comment at a time. But spread over a population of 8,000 plus, you get results that are right on the money.

Adding to the utility of the CIA and the Clusterizer is the ability to cross-index by sex, age, income, region, and a host of other variables. We might ask such a simple question as, "Where do you shop most often for women's dress clothes?" and cross-index the responses to find out what is the favorite dress-clothes shopping destination for urban women 34 to 40 with incomes of more than $40,000 who also shop Wal-Mart for groceries. I don't know why you would ask such a question, but with the Clusterizer and the CIA, you could do it.

What you can know is limited only by your imagination. And thanks to Internet technology, you can know it this morning and act on it right after lunch!

MIGRATION

If you knew which of your customers was the next one to leave, what would you do? Would it be helpful if you knew where they were going to make their next purchase and why? Could you act on that information? Well, yes, you could.

What you are about to read could easily be described as "radar for CEOs." Instead of waiting until the end of the quarter to discover that sales are down, you can know right now what is happening and take corrective action. The problem with financial documents is that they are always historical documents—helpful but always just a tad out-of-date.

With foreknowledge, you can see the future far enough out to change it!

One key tool for predicting future sales is the migration index. The migration index shows which companies are gaining customers and which are losing customers. It's reasonable to assume that customers are going to patronize different stores for the same general type of product or service. Influencing factors include promotions, convenience, even hours of operation.

Migration occurs when the consumer makes a conscious decision to change his or her primary retailer in the category for another. Look at the charts in this chapter and notice that there is both immigration and emigration (customers who are coming in on trial, others who are leaving for good.)

Analysts attempt to value companies using their customer base, the idea being that the more customers you have, the greater your potential sales. The key word is *potential*. But what if you have lots of customers (high value), but many of them are in the process of leaving? That would certainly paint an entirely different picture.

The migration index is based on three simple questions:

1. Where do you shop for X most often?
2. How long have you shopped there?
3. Where did you previously shop?

BIGresearch uses the Internet and asks thousands of people these questions each month. It's powerful stuff, but if you are an individual owner or manager, these are questions you can ask across the counter.

At our restaurant Sporty's, we play a variation on the theme by asking, "If Sporty's had not been a choice, where do you think you would have gone for lunch or dinner?"

Notice that the first question is, "Where do you shop for X?" where X equals a category, not a store. Why? Because no retailer owns 100 percent of the market for every category of product it carries. Imagine that it's late in the evening, and you decide to tinker with the lawn mower in your shop and discover it needs a quart of oil. At eight in the morning, you might head to the nearest Auto Zone, but at eight in the evening, you're thinking convenience; make it quick and make it easy.

On your way out the door you hear, "Honey! Can you pick up milk and blueberries while you're out?" (That came as a request, but it's really a command.) How do you refuse? "I'm only going for oil. You should have thought of it earlier." You could do that, but I wouldn't recommend it! Where can you get milk, blueberries, and motor oil that is open and close to home? The supermarket, of course. Or maybe there's a Super-Target just down the block.

If the manager of the Target were to notice your purchases, she might get the idea that her Target owns both your grocery business and your demand for automotive supplies. That would be logical, but it would also be flat out wrong. She could also notice that you have only grocery and automotive supplies and assume that she's not getting your purchases of sporting goods, consumer electronics, and women's wear. She could be wrong about this as well.

And that is precisely why we ask by category and not by store. By asking where you shop for X, we learn a customer's current favorite store for that category.

Next we ask, "How long have you been shopping there?" We want to know how, not just where, the customer is shopping. We want to know if this is a new customer or a long-term customer. Gaining lots of new customers is an indication that someone is losing them big time. So to really get a feel for customer migration, we have to look closely at new customers, typically those who have switched within the year.

The final question is, "Where did you shop for X previously?" This is the money question, because it tells us who is losing.

Customer Migration Precedes and Therefore Predicts Future Sales

Case in point: Kmart. Recently, Kmart reported a small profit, which is big news for the Big K—big news but not really great news. Why? Because our research told us that at the same time Kmart was reporting a profit for the first time in a long while, customers in several merchandise categories were telling us that they were abandoning ship.

Just for grins, I took a break to run the CIA for the current month. And, surprise, surprise, Kmart shoppers are telling us that over the next 90 days, they are planning to spend less in almost every category. Still, at the moment, most market analysts are calling for a Kmart comeback—but it ain't gonna happen.

Analysts Read Numbers; Smart Managers Read Customers

The statistical methods used by most market researchers today were developed in the late 1800s through 1950. Since then, there has been little change in the methods of either data collection or data analysis. Most old-line research is outdated the instant it is delivered: three months of fieldwork followed by three months of analysis equals old, semi-useless data.

Most retailers are using financial data to guide their businesses, which is fine, but not to the exclusion of talking to customers. Thanks to the Internet and the personal computer, you can do exactly that. The CRM (customer relationship management) folks use transaction data to tell you about your customers. Unfortunately, most of the data comes from credit card purchases, but less than 25 percent of all retail purchases are made by people using their own credit cards!

Financial data isn't going to cut it, nor will traditional market research do the job. *You have to talk to your customer!*

WATCHING THE MIGRATION INDEX

Unless you are in a town that is highly dependent on a single industry for employment, it's natural that some of your customers will move away, die, or outgrow their need for your product. But it is fair to worry when your net customer base begins to shrink. The migration index is just the indicator to watch.

The graphs we have selected in Figures 2.2, 2.3, and 2.4 are based on customers of one year or less. Be aware that we could just as easily have sorted for customers of any length of time, or we could have simply included all customers. We chose customers of one year or less as an example of one way to "cut" the data.

To help spot anomalies, we will examine the data "index" that expresses the magnitude of a datum point compared to the average. Here it comes in English: An index of 100 is average. If something has an index of 50, then that something is occurring at a rate that is half the av-

FIGURE 2.2 *Home Improvement/Hardware Store Migration, June 2003–June 2004*

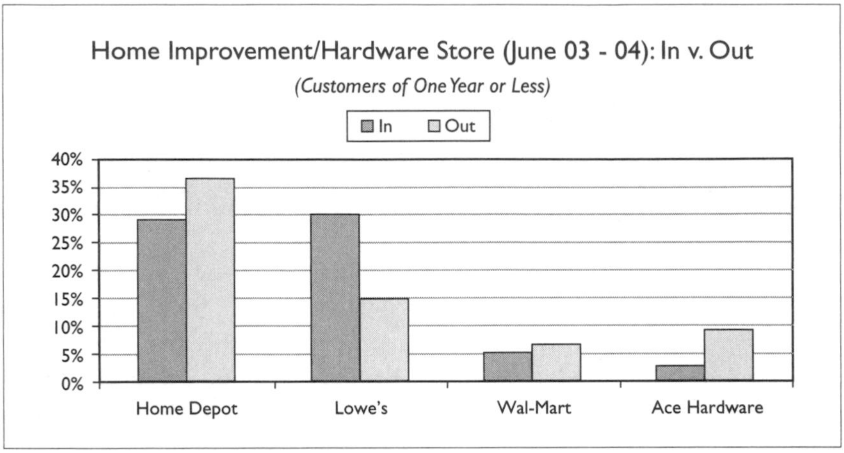

Home Improvement/Hardware Store (June 03 - 04): In v. Out
(Customers of One Year or Less)

Legend: ■ In   □ Out

Source: BIGresearch, Consumer Intentions and Actions, June 2004.

erage. An index of 200 means the rate of appearance is twice that of the average.

If the average height of a human male is 68 inches (index is 100), then a male who is 73 inches has a height index of 107. A male of only 62 inches in height would have an index of 91. The index is a good way to compare a datum point against the average, and it is a great way to spot anomalies when viewing lots of data.

According to the migration index, it's easy to see that Lowe's is the big winner, and that Home Depot, Wal-Mart, and Ace Hardware are taking it in the chops. But this doesn't signal game over. We're only talking one month out of forever. It could be that Lowe's had a killer promotion, or maybe that the other guys got complacent. If I were Home Depot, would I worry? You bet! Would I give up? No way! But I would ask to see more of the data, and there is plenty more to be seen.

The two obvious questions are, Why are newer customers leaving Home Depot? and What about the competition (Lowe's) is so attractive? Are customers going to Lowe's or running from Home Depot? And who is making the move?

The answer can be found, purse over shoulder, wandering around the appliance department—women! Look at the chart in Figure 2.3 comparing Home Depot and Lowe's for home improvement and hardware categories, and you'll see that the companies look remarkably similar in terms of average age and income. Look at the other numbers, and you begin to see that Home Depot customers are less likely to be married, and that Lowe's customers are a bit more touchy-feely. The Lowe's shop-

FIGURE 2.3 *Home Depot versus Lowe's Appliance*

	Home Depot	Lowe's	Index
What is your gender?			
Male	53.6%	41.2%	130
Female	46.4%	58.8%	79
Total	100.0%	100.0%	
What is your marital status?			
Married	48.6%	68.5%	71
Living with unmarried partner	10.1%	9.4%	107
Divorced or separated	13.1%	8.4%	156
Widowed	4.5%	3.1%	143
Single, never married	23.8%	10.5%	226
Total	100.0%	100.0%	
Please tell us which age range you are in:			
18–24	14.1%	7.7%	183
25–34	21.7%	16.5%	132
35–44	23.8%	25.7%	93
45–54	15.1%	20.3%	74
55–64	10.9%	14.6%	75
65+	14.3%	15.2%	94
Total	100.0%	100.0%	
Average Age	42.7	45.9	93
What is the annual total income of your household?			
Less than $15,000	15.4%	7.5%	204
$15,000 to $24,999	6.5%	15.5%	42
$25,000 to $34,999	12.7%	16.5%	77
$35,000 to $49,999	31.9%	18.6%	171
$50,000 to $74,999	14.0%	24.1%	58
$75,000 to $99,999	13.0%	10.7%	121
$100,000 to $149,999	4.9%	5.9%	83
$150,000 or more	1.7%	1.1%	145
Total	100.0%	100.0%	
Average Income	$49,363	$50,524	98
In the last six months, have you made any of the following changes? (Check all that apply.)			
I have become more practical and realistic in my purchases.	44.5%	47.5%	94
I focus more on what I NEED rather than what I WANT.	53.2%	60.6%	88
I am spending more time and money on decorating my home.	15.0%	15.8%	95

(continued)

FIGURE 2.3 *Home Depot versus Lowe's Appliance (Continued)*

	Home Depot	Lowe's	Index
In the last six months, have you made any of the following changes? (Check all that apply.)			
I worry more about political and national security issues.	24.1%	25.8%	94
I have reordered priorities in my daily life.	30.5%	26.5%	115
I have reordered my priorities in my professional/working life.	19.7%	11.2%	176
I am spending more time with my family.	30.0%	31.0%	97
I have not made any changes.	19.0%	19.2%	99
Which statement best describes you regarding home improvement? (Check only one.)			
Regular "do-it-yourselfer" (DIYer)—helps others	16.0%	14.2%	112
Regular DIYer	19.1%	18.0%	106
Regular DIYer—needs to do research	25.9%	18.4%	141
No time to do home projects	26.9%	30.0%	90
No interest in doing home projects	12.1%	19.4%	63
Total	100.0%	100.0%	
Which room(s) are you planning to improve? (Check all that apply.)			
Basement/Rec Room	10.9%	3.3%	336
Bathroom	25.1%	28.9%	87
Bedroom	24.2%	27.5%	88
Deck/Porch	22.7%	21.1%	108
Den/Study	6.2%	6.1%	102
Kitchen	27.7%	36.0%	77
Living Room	14.6%	26.4%	56
Other	31.6%	31.8%	99

The sum of the percent totals may be greater than 100 percent because the respondents can select more than one answer.

Source: BIGresearch, Consumer Intentions and Actions, June 2004.

per is more interested in new styles, design, and even the appearance and layout of the store.

The real difference between Lowe's and Home Depot is in the appliance department. This customer is decidedly more likely to be female, married, and focused on needs rather than wants. So what is she doing shopping for new appliances? She's older by a few years, which likely means her appliances are older as well. Even though the compulsion to shop has not disappeared, the new focus on need versus want

FIGURE 2.4 *Home Depot versus Lowe's Home Improvement/Hardware*

	Home Depot	Lowe's	Index
What is your gender?			
Male	46.7%	46.1%	101
Female	53.3%	53.9%	99
Total	100.0%	100.0%	
What is your marital status?			
Married	54.8%	62.9%	87
Living with unmarried partner	8.7%	8.8%	98
Divorced or separated	12.1%	10.6%	114
Widowed	4.7%	3.2%	149
Single, never married	19.7%	14.5%	136
Total	100.0%	100.0%	
Please tell us which age range you are in:			
18–24	10.4%	8.5%	121
25–34	16.9%	18.4%	92
35–44	23.5%	22.4%	105
45–54	18.6%	21.5%	86
55–64	12.6%	13.6%	93
65+	18.1%	15.6%	116
Total	100.0%	100.0%	
Average Age	45.7	45.6	100
What is the annual total income of your household?			
Less than $15,000	8.2%	9.6%	85
$15,000 to $24,999	11.5%	13.0%	88
$25,000 to $34,999	15.7%	16.5%	95
$35,000 to $49,999	21.8%	19.5%	112
$50,000 to $74,999	23.0%	24.0%	96
$75,000 to $99,999	11.1%	9.4%	118
$100,000 to $149,999	6.5%	6.4%	101
$150,000 or more	2.2%	1.4%	150
Total	100.0%	100.0%	
Average Income	$53,136	$50,627	105
What are the reasons you buy your home improvement/hardware items there? (Check all that apply.)			
Price	76.9%	77.0%	100
Selection	81.9%	82.2%	100
Location	71.0%	66.0%	108
Quality	53.2%	56.7%	94
Service	38.1%	42.1%	90

(continued)

FIGURE 2.4 *Home Depot versus Lowe's Home Improvement/Hardware (Continued)*

	Home Depot	Lowe's	Index
What are the reasons you buy your home improvement/hardware items there? (Check all that apply.)			
Financing options	4.7%	5.2%	90
Store appearance	11.5%	18.5%	62
Store layout	17.8%	26.5%	67
Home Improvement ideas/tips	30.5%	27.7%	110
Newest styles/products	13.9%	16.2%	86
Installation services	10.2%	11.2%	92
Knowledgeable salespeople	34.7%	30.8%	113
Other	2.4%	2.9%	81

The sum of the percent totals may be greater than 100 percent because the respondents can select more than one answer.

Source: BIGresearch, Consumer Intentions and Actions, June 2004.

comes in balance in the appliance department: "I want something new, and what could be more practical than a washer-dryer or a new double-side fridge?"

And now that we are spending more time with the family, jazzing up the kitchen makes sense. Lowe's listened when customers talked, and now they are one of the fastest-growing retailers of appliances in America, and Home Depot has some catching up to do.

Now let's spend some time in women's clothing. A quick glance at the migration index in Figure 2.5 prompts this question, "Why do losses from Sears and JCPenney seem to be so much greater than the gains at Wal-Mart?" It's simple. All the players are not shown on the board. While some of loss from Sears undoubtedly was Wal-Mart's gain, the rest went to Kohl's, Steinmart, specialty boutiques, and others.

If I were Sears, I would want to know why customers are leaving and what makes Wal-Mart so attractive. By the way, if you are working at Sears, there is a good chance you won't recognize the problem. Logically, you may think, "We have more comfortable stores, better selection, and higher quality at a competitive price. Why would someone not shop with us?"

Well, let's find out!

FIGURE 2.5 *Women's Clothing Store Migration, May 2003–May 2004*

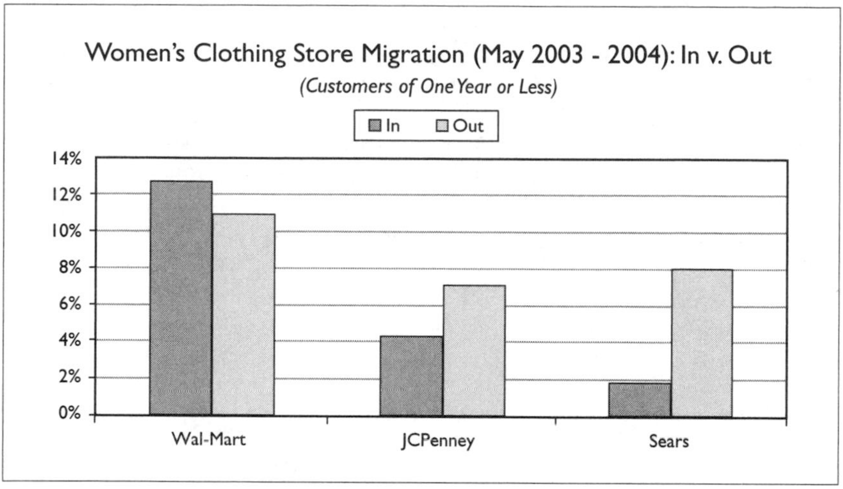

Women's Clothing Store Migration (May 2003 - 2004): In v. Out
(Customers of One Year or Less)

Source: BIGresearch, Consumer Intentions and Actions, May 2004.

Here's a quick quiz. When it comes to women's clothes, which is more important, fashion or value? Quick quiz, part 2: Which is the most important factor when women purchase clothes, price or quality? Quick quiz, part 3: Women prefer conservative clothes, true or false?

Clothing brands have little meaning when 64.1 percent report familiar clothing labels are unimportant. (See Figure 2.6.) About the same number, 62 percent, say they are more concerned about value and comfort than fashion. And watch this—67.8 percent usually buy clothing when it's on sale, while another 19.7 percent say they only buy on deal. Put them together, and 87.5 percent of the market is zeroed in on the clearance rack.

When you think price, do you think Sears? When you think fashion, do you think Wal-Mart? Well, there you have it. The women of America are going for the made-in-China, elastic waistband, polyester pants, and they *still* aren't buying unless they're on the sale rack or at Wal-Mart, where they promise everyday low prices.

If Sears is going to attract the women's clothing shopper, it's going to have to promote value, maybe better quality at a slightly higher price but value nonetheless.

Finally, someone is eating Wal-Mart's lunch! But it isn't Kmart, JCPenney, or Sears. Who is it and why? Digging in the data, we find what might account for the odd-looking graph in Figure 2.7 on page 24. When asked about shopping habits, customers told us that giant, enclosed regional malls may be losing ground to freestanding stores and

FIGURE 2.6 *Survey Says . . .*

	Female (18+)	Kohl's	JC Penney	Sears	Target	Wal-Mart	Specialty Store	Dept. Store
Respondents Selected:	5,513	351	398	142	187	1,495	903	1,616

What are the reasons you buy your Women's Clothing there? (Check all that apply.)

	Female (18+)	Kohl's	JC Penney	Sears	Target	Wal-Mart	Specialty Store	Dept. Store
Price	80.3%	94.8%	80.4%	85.1%	95.4%	96.2%	70.8%	81.2%
Selection	68.6%	84.2%	82.1%	81.7%	65.7%	55.7%	81.1%	81.2%
Location	49.3%	58.8%	50.2%	54.5%	61.1%	63.6%	39.2%	54.2%
Quality	51.1%	63.1%	69.3%	67.0%	49.6%	34.5%	59.0%	69.2%
Service	20.8%	24.6%	21.7%	26.7%	20.4%	17.3%	23.8%	25.3%
Fashion ideas	16.4%	14.3%	9.7%	10.4%	14.4%	9.4%	30.2%	13.3%
Newest styles	18.1%	21.2%	12.3%	11.8%	15.9%	9.3%	31.8%	18.3%
Newest fabrics	7.2%	7.3%	2.9%	7.3%	6.4%	4.1%	13.4%	6.5%
Knowledgeable salespeople	8.6%	5.3%	8.4%	7.3%	5.8%	5.7%	13.0%	10.4%
Other	7.0%	1.4%	6.6%	4.3%	4.3%	4.1%	14.6%	4.8%

How have fluctuating gas prices impacted your spending? (Check all that apply.)

Delayed major purchase such as car, TV, furniture	15.0%
Reduced dining out	26.3%
Decreased vacation/travel	33.6%
Increased carpooling	5.2%
Spending less on groceries	15.2%
Spending less on clothing	20.5%
Other	8.9%
No major impact	42.7%

When buying clothes, familiar labels are important to me.

Yes	35.9%
No	64.1%
Total	100.0%

Check the statement that best applies to your feelings about fashion. (Check only one.)

Newest trends and styles are important to me.	8.5%
I prefer a traditional conservative look.	29.5%
Fashion is less important than value and comfort to me.	62.0%
Total	100.0%

Which one of the following best describes your shopping strategy for clothing? (Check only one.)

Sales are not important to me when buying clothing.	12.5%
I usually buy clothing when it's on sale.	67.8%
I only buy clothing when it's on sale.	19.7%
Total	100.0%

FIGURE 2.6 *Survey Says . . (Continued)*

Women's clothing (shop at most often)	
Department store	22.5%
Discount store	26.3%
Specialty—apparel	11.2%
Membership warehouse	0.2%
Catalog	1.2%
Internet	0.2%
Other	5.5%
No preference	32.8%
Total	100.0%

The sum of the percent totals may be greater than 100 percent because the respondents can select more than one answer.

Source: BIGresearch, Consumer Intentions and Actions, May 2004.

strip centers, which is exactly where you are most likely to find Bed Bath & Beyond.

If there is a surprise, it is that Wal-Mart is beginning to slip. Why? Asked "What are the reasons behind your linens/bedding/drapery purchases?" shoppers listed the following reasons (and, just for fun, we'll see what women say about clothes):

Linens/Bedding		Women's Clothes	
Price	69.2%	Price	80.3%
Selection	48.9%	Selection	68.6%
Location	36.0%	Location	49.3%
Quality	37.7%	Quality	51.1%

Notice that price is less of an issue when it comes to linens versus clothes. Selection, while important, is also not that big a deal. Location and quality are also less of a consideration. The thinking must be that since price and quality aren't such huge issues, we might as well make the trip fast and easy and head to a local strip center where Bed, Bath, and Beyond rules the roost.

If you were Bed Bath & Beyond, how would you shape your marketing? You might definitely want to mention convenient shopping right in the neighborhood. Maybe you could snatch even more of Wally World's customers!

Electronics is a huge category that is only going to get bigger as competition forces margins lower. (See Figure 2.8.) Without looking at the

FIGURE 2.7 *Linen/Bedding/Draperies Store Migration, April 2003–April 2004*

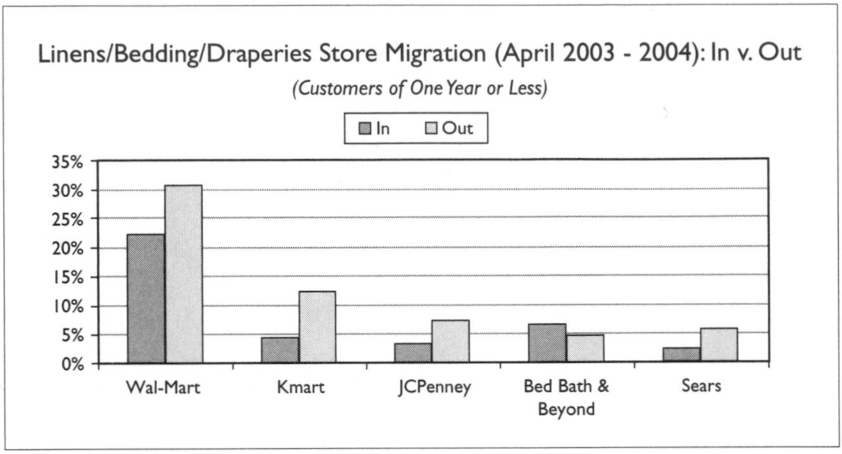

Source: BIGresearch, Consumer Intentions and Actions, April 2004.

numbers, I know that this is a price-sensitive category. Why is it that Wal-Mart and Best Buy are able to take such a big bite out of Circuit City and Sears? If I were Circuit City, I would want to know where my customers went and why they decided to leave:

Circuit City		Best Buy		Wal-Mart	
Price	83.7%	Price	90.4%	Price	96.0%
Selection	79.4%	Selection	59.8%	Selection	51.1%
Location	56.5%	Location	54.1%	Location	59.6%
Quality	56.6%	Quality	53.2%	Quality	32.7%

It's price. Look at the numbers. Customers shop Circuit City for the selection, while Wal-Mart and Best Buy customers are looking for the deal. The question that Circuit City may want to consider is, "Can we beat the competition at their game (price), or should we take another tactic and wow the market with selection?"

Notice that Wal-Mart customers aren't too concerned about quality. Either they expect quality to not be an issue or perhaps they figure the life of the product will be so short that maintenance won't matter. Circuit City's most direct competitor is Best Buy. If you were Circuit City, how would you position your company? How about "Great prices on the things you want"?

The prescription drug store migration is a puzzle until you take a deeper look. (See Figure 2.9.) Who would imagine that Wal-Mart would be losing share among customers of one year or less? Rite Aid and Eckerd we can casually chalk up to natural competitive forces, but Wal-Mart?

FIGURE 2.8 *Electronics Store Migration, March 2003–March 2004*

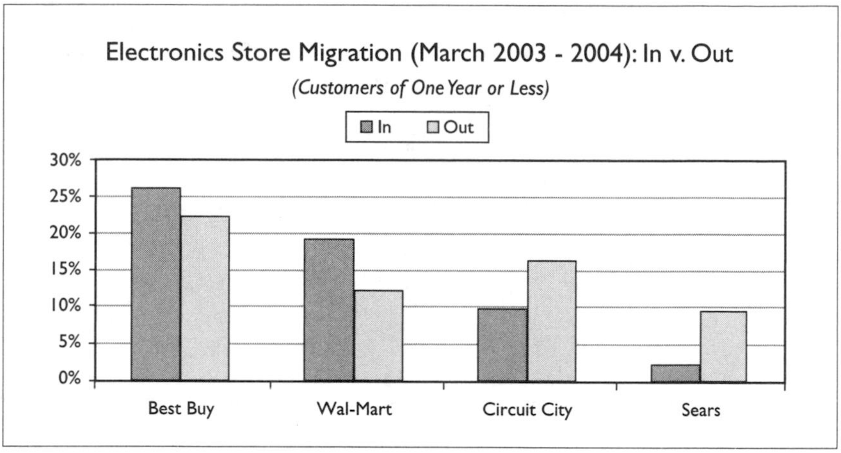

Electronics Store Migration (March 2003 - 2004): In v. Out
(Customers of One Year or Less)

Source: BIGresearch, Consumer Intentions and Actions, March 2004.

Look at the reasons shoppers cite as determining factors when purchasing prescription drugs. Pay attention! We're not talking shampoo and makeup remover pads. We're talking prescription drugs:

Location	64.9%
Prescriptions covered by insurance	44.8%
Prescriptions phoned in	42.6%
Price	36.2%

Compared to location, price comes in a distant fourth, or perhaps a not-so-close second, if you consider being covered by insurance an element of price.

Location, which could be translated as convenience, is the major factor in the purchase of prescription drugs. Wal-Mart simply cannot put a Supercenter in every neighborhood, even if it seems like they already have! But Walgreens and CVS, with their much smaller stores and the ability to use smaller parcels of land, is beating Wal-Mart at a different game. Particularly when you are not feeling well, convenience becomes a huge competitive advantage.

Rather than pitching price, Walgreens and CVS are pitching convenience, something Wal-Mart isn't set up to provide—yet. Wal-Mart has started building smaller "neighborhood" stores. If they aren't already everywhere, they will be.

FIGURE 2.9 *Prescription Drug Store Migration, February 2003–February 2004*

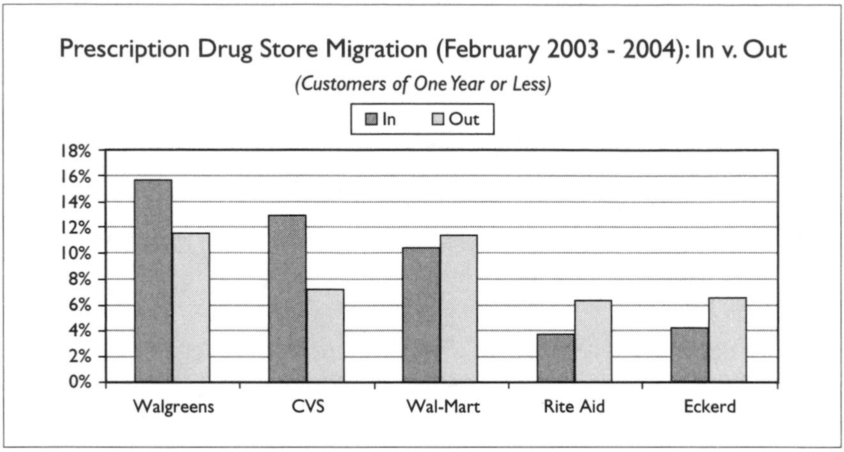

Prescription Drug Store Migration (February 2003 - 2004): In v. Out
(Customers of One Year or Less)

Source: BIGresearch, Consumer Intentions and Actions, February 2004.

CREATURES OF HABIT

If you don't think customers are creatures of habit, try running a restaurant for a day or two. It won't take long to discover that customers really are creatures of habit. Once they lock onto a menu item, there isn't much that will change their minds.

What keeps customers coming back is one simple idea—comfort. Customer behavior is governed by the prospect of feeling good. They go where they are made to feel good. They buy what they think will make them feel good. Sometimes, the very act of buying or shopping is driven by the need to feel good.

Buns, my wife, measures her sense of normalcy by the ability to spend one day out of each month rummaging through consignment shops and strolling the mall in search of bargains. She doesn't have to actually buy something to feel good. For others, it is the act of purchasing that gives a sense of comfort. Buns and I went to an estate sale and were appalled to see that the deceased woman had hundreds of dresses, cookbooks, and hardware items still with price tags. For her, shopping was pathological in that she felt compelled to purchase.

Sometimes, shopping is done from the obverse side of the coin: the need to avoid feeling bad. Try telling a teenager that he looks funny with his pants riding low and underwear showing. He knows he looks ridiculous, but not looking like his friends is such an uncomfortable thought that regular pants are out of the question.

Our motives are often simple to the point of stupidity. We may stop at a fast-food joint where we know the food is awful, but it is the only place still open and we are feeling hungry. I want to feel good or I just don't want to feel bad. That's all the explanation necessary to understand buyers' motivations.

When we create marketing campaigns and materials, we know where we want the market to go. We know what we want the market to buy. What we too often fail to ask is, "Where does the customer shop now?" and "What is the customer actually buying?" In Chapter 6, we'll show you what you need to know to take advantage of existing customer habits, while at the same time creating new habits that will work for you!

The focus of all marketing should be trial that results in a sale. Advertising moves product, and marketing changes habit.

For most retailers, organized sales efforts revolve around two words, *discount* and *bundle*. In the minds of most consumers, the discounted, or sales, price has come to represent the actual value of the product. Then there is the delusion that the actual price of a signature product can be disguised by bundling it with accessory items, so that the package looks like a bargain while the signature item retains full value in the mind of the consumer.

That's nonsense. *Discount* is a fancy term for "give stuff away," and *bundle* is a French term meaning "give more stuff away."

How do you know when to discount? Sorry, there is no simple answer to this question, unless you are willing to accept, "It depends." Here are the top influences of the purchase decision for three very different categories of product:

Electronics		New Vehicle		Skin Care/Cosmetics	
Price	77.4%	High miles	35.0%	It works	52.7%
Selection	59.8%	Tired of old	30.1%	Quality	49.0%
Location	46.5%	Incentives	20.7%	Price	47.0%
Quality	40.5%	Unreliable	19.7%	Comfort	33.3%
Service	30.5%	Better mpg	18.2%	On sale	25.2%
Help	20.5%	New style	17.3%	Special deal	24.0%

It won't be easy to sell electronics at a premium. It's tough to sell a new car if the old car is still running fine. And cosmetics that don't make you think you look good are staying on the shelf. Price, necessity, and vanity—three products with three disparate motivators.

Tune In

Take a look at the reasons behind the purchase decision for electronics. Notice the strong focus on price. Quality, while important, weighs in at number four. Why? Because quality is no longer an issue in electronics. Buy a CD player, a cell phone, or a digital camera, and you can pretty much bet that you will lose it before you break it, or it will become outdated before it wears out. Electronics are so price-competitive that even location made it near the top of the list. The thinking seems to be, "They're all about the same price, so just stop at the nearest store."

Knowledgeable sales help barely made the list for electronics purchases, but they are nowhere to be seen under new vehicle or cosmetics. Because of the rapid advances in technology, consumers still want a little advice when making their selections. As electronics become more and more intuitive, as they become more plug-and-play, and as the devices themselves take on a greater role in their own installation, knowledgeable sales staff will slide peacefully off the list.

Motivated to Buy

Look at the motivators behind new car purchases. The surest way to turn out a new car buyer is to convince her that the old car is unreliable. Among the top four motivators, three have to do with age and reliability—high miles on the old car, tired of the old car, and old car in the shop too often.

New styling has relatively little to do with the purchase decision. Combined average fuel economy regulations have forced manufacturers to adopt look-alike body shapes. New electronic technology is no longer the domain of the newly wealthy. You can put XM radio and GPS navigation in a Kia just as easily as in a BMW. New engine and body technology has greatly improved reliability. Who needs a new car? Gone are the days when "old car rusted through" might have been a serious car purchase motivation!

Turn On

Finally, check out reasons behind cosmetic purchases. When you look at the reasons cited, it seems there are only two. First, it makes me feel good, and second, I got it on deal. It works, quality, and comfortable are all ways of saying, "This makes me look and feel good." Reasons three, five, and six are all about price. If you look at the entire list of responses, you'll see other price-related motivators, such as gift with purchase, two for one, and coupon.

ACTING ON FOREKNOWLEDGE

There is no single formula for selling every product to any customer. You have to find out *why* they buy, and that only happens when customers talk. A wise person we can't find said: "Anybody can give away product. It takes brains to sell it." Keep reading and we'll show you how.

You might define *foreknowledge* as discovering what the customer thinks before the customer acts. The biggest obstacle to foreknowledge is being stuck in old thinking and failing to ask the questions that could pay, if only we had the imagination to ask.

What this country doesn't need is another new product. But need isn't what we sell; we sell want. The old model works like this: A manufacturer creates a new product and peddles it to retailers—no test or trial, just new product at an attractive price, no clear demand. But stocking product for which there is no demand is a retailer's nightmare. What if we could test new thinking almost overnight? If we could, we could make new product decisions confidently and still easily be first to market.

An international retailer asked BIGresearch to test a private-label cola. There's really no way to taste-test online; that's still left to old-fashioned shoe leather technology. But you can test brand names, packaging, pricing, and marketing. And you can do it almost overnight!

Online surveying might be useful to clothing buyers. The old-fashioned way to buy clothing is to wait for the fashion mavens in New York and Paris to pronounce what's hot, or not, buy as best you can, and wait. If it works, you are a hero; if not, blame it on the weather and hope for better results next year.

What if you asked the customer what *she* wanted to wear? What if you could learn what is hot or not directly from the customer? Consumer research is most valuable when it tells us what *not* to buy. Retailers don't get hurt when they guess correctly. Not buying merchandise that doesn't sell prevents low or no margin sales primarily designed to close the books on buying mistakes.

The National Retail Federation uses CIA (Consumer Intentions and Actions) to assist retailers and Wall Street in making intelligent decisions in various selling seasons. If you want to know what the customer is going to do, who is the most logical person to ask, an economist or a customer?

What if you could know 60 to 90 days in advance which products were most likely to fly off the shelf and which were likely to gather dust? Could you stop the freighter that had already sailed from China? Unfortunately, no. But what you can do is adjust your pricing and marketing strategies. Knowing, having foreknowledge, is of little value unless you are willing to be flexible and adjust your plan.

Not only will customers tell you what will sell, they also will tell you how much they will buy and how they intend to pay for it. If you could know this, *and you can,* do you think you might adjust your in-store credit card program, think about financing options, and perhaps consider product mix?

Foreknowledge truly is radar for CEOs.

3

THE BIG IDEA

If Sergeant Joe Friday of the 1950s TV show *Dragnet* was on the case, he would want the facts, just the facts. Sergeant Friday would want to see BIGresearch in action before he would ever risk making a move. So here are some facts that you and the good sergeant can chew on.

CONSUMER CONFIDENCE

On May 28, 2004, the *Wall Street Journal* reported that consumer confidence slipped an even 4 percent from April to May. But on May 14, exactly two weeks earlier, using a slightly different scale, BIGresearch released the BIG Executive Briefing, which announced that consumer confidence continued to flutter in the 45–46 percent range, with a 1.5 point decline from April to 45.1 percent in May.

In other words, BIGresearch customers had a two-week planning head start on the competition. When companies have foreknowledge, they know where the consumers and the economy are headed.

HERMENEUTICAL ANALYSIS

If you have read this far, I am certain that you cannot believe I would have a section titled "Hermeneutical Analysis." It wasn't my idea. It was one of my coauthors' ideas. In fact, Joe wanted me to remind you that "the dialogic model of the interview locates the actors as partners in a situation (here) who are oriented by the topic-of-concern (there). The actors share a temporally present situation that emerges from a convergence of their biological (past) life and the reciprocal expectations of what is behaviorally possible in the future."

Well, excuuuse me! What was that all about? Thank you, Professor Pilotta!

I shall interpret. What Joe really wanted to say is that scientific interviewers (pollsters included) try not to influence the response of the people they are surveying. On the surface this makes sense. If you allow your personal biases to shape the responses, isn't that a bit like interviewing yourself?

Well, apparently there is another way to look at it, and that's where the idea of hermeneutics comes in. (We won't use that word again, so relax.) Maybe, goes the theory, it might be as well to include the interviewer as a social participant. Let the interviewer interact with the folks who are being polled.

That sounds like a bad idea until you go a little deeper. Language is not simply a matter of words strung together to express a thought. Language is much more than simple words. Language consists of words delivered in the cultural context of the speaker, further colored by the cultural context of the receiver. (Ohmygosh . . . I've caught something from Joe!)

Interviewer and interviewee alike bring presuppositions to the interview. Joe says, rather than attempt the impossibility of eliminating preconceptions, we should be aware of them and consider them as a factor when interpreting polling results. You can't fully understand any response until it is put in context anyway. So rather than attempting to eliminate social or cultural bias, the smart researcher will consider it in the interpretation.

"Presuppositions," according to Joe, "aren't problems at all, so long as we are aware of them. In fact, they help us gain a common understanding."

While good customer interviews do not unnecessarily influence the respondent, respondents definitely influence the direction of a well-constructed interview. A culturally sensitive interviewer will be able to detect the slightest of nuances and create follow-up questions likely to increase the data haul immensely. For example:

"How did you enjoy your meal tonight?"

"It was okay."

What does that mean? Well, you and I both know that phrased as, "It was okay," implies it definitely was not okay! If there were no room for interviewer discretion, an answer of "It was okay" could easily pass as a positive response and fail to lead us to probe deeper.

It is the responsibility of the interviewer to collect data *and* give it meaning. Otherwise, there is a high risk that facts collected will be accurate but useless.

A question is always from a person, but an answer is not always to a question. In many, if not most cases, an answer is to the anticipated response of the questioner. In other words, the questioner may have so much influence on the answer that the answer is worthless without interpretation.

Our German shepherd Bailey is notorious for answering questions based on the context in which they are asked. Look her in the eye and announce, "Who wants . . . " and, before you can complete the sentence, she will leap to her feet and act. If it is in the morning and I am standing near the stove, she will race to the pantry in anticipation of hearing, "Who wants an egg?"

But stand near the stove, opening a carton of eggs and announce, "Who wants to go for a ride?" and the poor girl won't know which way to turn! Answers are greatly influenced by the questioner and the context in which they are asked. The criticism of online scientific surveying is its lack of context and inability to detect nuance.

Without cultural context, it may be impossible to accurately interpret any human polling data. Did consumers rush out and purchase new household appliances because they thought the economy was good or out of fear of a looming shortage? That's context.

All data is interpreted data, if not by the gatherer, at least by the respondent. Or, as Joe might say it, "Phenomenologically speaking, a sociohistorically acquired understanding is a fundamental mode of interpreting phenomena." I think what he means is, "The customer will always interpret the meaning of your questions in his or her terms."

RISING GAS PRICES AND SUV SALES

On May 19, 2004, the *Wall Street Journal* announced that GM, Ford, and DaimlerChrysler had "ratcheted up discounts on their largest and

FIGURE 3.1   *Vehicle Sales Being Considered, January 2004–May 2004*

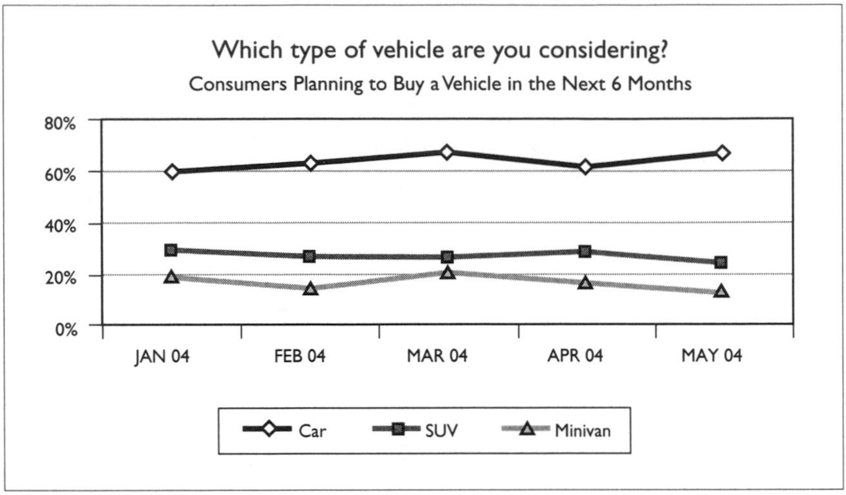

Which type of vehicle are you considering?
Consumers Planning to Buy a Vehicle in the Next 6 Months

Source: BIGresearch, Consumer Intentions and Actions, May 2004.

least-fuel-efficient models in hopes of moving out a glut of unsold pick-ups and sport-utility vehicles." Should they have seen what was coming? Could they?

We did. Two months earlier, in March, fewer consumers were telling us they had plans to purchase SUVs and minivans in the next six months, while more and more were saying they might move to more-fuel-efficient cars. In January, consumers began to tell us that in the next six months, of those with purchase intentions, more were planning to buy cars (66.7 percent in May versus 59.3 percent in January), and fewer were intending to purchase an SUV (23.4 percent versus 28.4 percent in January) or a minivan (12.8 percent versus 18.9 percent in January). (See Figure 3.1.)

CIA May 2004—Executive Briefing Excerpt

Rising prices at the pump were all over the news and were expected to go higher during the summer months. How was this affecting consumer spending? When comparing different incomes, it appeared that rising fuel prices were having more of an effect on households earning under $50,000 annually than on those bringing home over $50,000 (52.9 percent of those earning more than $50,000 said no major impact versus only 38.1 percent of under-$50,000 wage earners). Check out Figure 3.2 for a clearer picture on who was cutting back (and who wasn't).

FIGURE 3.2 *Effect of Rising Gas Prices on Consumer Spending*

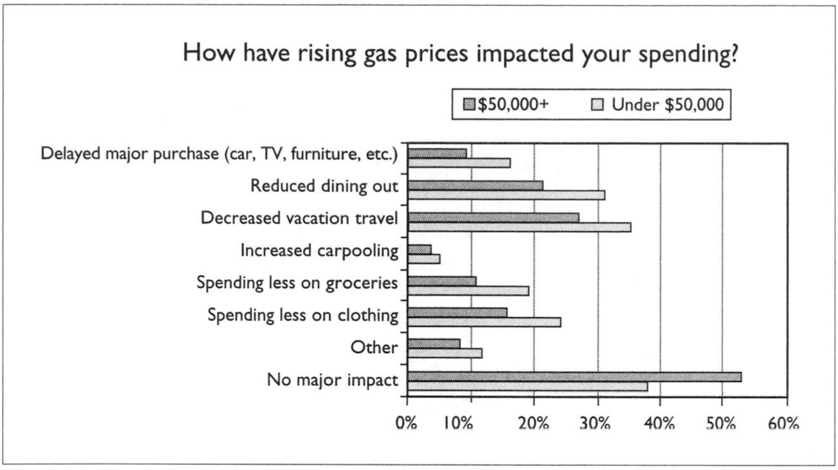

How have rising gas prices impacted your spending?

Source: BIGresearch, Consumer Intentions and Actions, May 2004.

Spending over Memorial Day weekend looked like it would be affected by higher pump prices as well (42.2 percent of under-$50,000 households predicted gas prices would impact spending versus 31.8 percent of over-$50,000 households).

When taking a look at who might be cutting back spending on clothing or household items because of the increasing cost of gas, it looked like discount stores (shopped more often by lower-income households) like Wal-Mart, Kmart, and Target would be affected more than their department and specialty store competition. Compared to the responses of all consumers (noted in parenthesis in Figure 3.3), those planning to cut back on clothing shopped discount stores more often than average.

To be read as: Of those consumers who said they were cutting back apparel expenditures as a result of high gas prices, 28.3 percent shop at Wal-Mart most often for women's clothing. The 19.2 percent represents the percentage of all consumers who shop at Wal-Mart most often for women's clothing.

Gas Hikes "Steal Share of Wallet" from Other Products/Services

Rising prices at the pump are a harsh reality that will not end soon. In fact, even if the Saudis were to increase their output, as was speculated in the news, resulting lower prices for auto fuel would probably not occur until the fall of 2004, and even then would not drop significantly.

FIGURE 3.3 *Effect of Gas Prices on Expected Clothing and Household Purchases*

Women's Clothing	Men's Clothing	Children's Clothing	Shoes	Linens
1. Wal-Mart 28.3% (19.2%)	1. Wal-Mart 36.3% (22.8%)	1. Wal-Mart 27.2% (17.4%)	1. Wal-Mart 26.9% (17.0%)	1. Wal-Mart 38.5% (26.7%)
2. JCPenney 6.6% (6.3%)	2. JCPenney 6.6% (8.4%)	2. Target 4.6% (3.5%)	2. Payless 21.9% (18.7%)	2. JCPenney 8.3% (8.7%)
3. Kohl's 4.3% (4.9%)	3. Sears 4.2% (4.5%)	3. Kmart 2.5% (1.7%)	3. Kmart 4.7% (3.1%)	3. Kmart 4.9% (3.6%)
4. Kmart 3.0% (2.2%)	4. Kohl's 3.7% (5.1%)	4. JCPenney 2.3% (2.6%)	4. JCPenney 2.5% (2.8%)	4. Linens 'n Things 4.4% (4.2%)
5. Target 2.5% (2.5%)	5. Kmart 3.5% (3.0%)	5. Kohl's 2.0% (2.1%)	5. Sears 2.4% (2.6%)	(tie) Target 4.4% (4.7%)
(tie) Sears 2.5% (2.3%)	(tie) Target 3.5% (2.7%)	(tie) Sears 2.0% (1.8%)		6. Bed Bath & Beyond 3.8% (6.6%)

Source: BIGresearch. To be read as: Of those consumers who said they were cutting back apparel expenditures as a result of high gas prices, 28.3 percent shop at Wal-Mart most often for women's clothing. The 19.2 percent represents the percentage of all consumers who shop at Wal-Mart most often for women's clothing.

This phenomenon obviously impacts consumer spending behavior, with fuel representing more of a necessity than many other needs and/ or wants. Of course, behavior does differ between earning levels (as seen in Figure 3.2).

Sectors to Be Most Affected by Gas Prices

Unfortunately, just as Wal-Mart's size and competitive success factors are positive levers for increasing business, their size and share of market can also work against them, as is the case with gas price hikes. Not only does the discount sector fare worse than the department and specialty store sectors in all categories, in each major apparel category (see Figure 3.3), a much larger percentage of consumers cutting back on clothing spending shopped at Wal-Mart, compared to average. Given the fact that the discount channel is shopped more often by lower-income households, and Wal-Mart's majority share of that channel, the gas hike impact was not surprising.

As value-driven consumers are forced to steal from their Wal-Mart shopping dollars to pay higher gas prices, they will likely react in two ways:

1. Cut back on their shopping frequency to Wal-Mart.
2. Cut back on nonfood purchases in Wal-Mart.

CEO Lee Scott estimated recently that higher gas prices have led to a $7 decrease each week in the average consumer's disposable income. To lessen the impact on consumers' wallets, a "good citizen" concept such as a Summer Gas Rebate promotion, declaring Wal-Mart's ongoing commitment to add value to the communities they serve, could be perceived as a "nonsale" to consumers, indeed confirming Wal-Mart's #1 ranking as giver to their communities. *(End of BIGresearch commentary)*

IF CUSTOMERS ONLY KNEW. . .

This is a tale of two companies, one that puts the customer first and one that has lost its way.

The commuter plane slipped smoothly to the runway. Little puffs of blue smoke were the only proof the tires of the main gear had finally made contact with the ribbon of asphalt welcoming us to Bentonville.

"It's so small," was all I could think. There was nothing more than a tiny building, too small to be labeled a terminal. No wonder so many Wal-Mart suitors elect to fly into Little Rock and load into a rental car for the last leg of the trip.

It had been years since I first made the trip, but I'd been told that not much had changed. Vendors by the dozen were invited, make that "allowed," to cram themselves into one of a hundred or so cheap plastic chairs to wait for an audience with a Wal-Mart buyer. First you registered at the reception desk, then shifted from one cheek to the other in the plastic chair, and finally your name was called along with a room assignment.

Vendors marched down a long hallway, some dreaming of the big sale, that once-in-a-lifetime score that would, or at least could, send a small-time operator with a big idea straight into the big league. At least that was the thought, the dream, but rarely the reality. I remember that hallway as stretching for miles, although a hundred or so feet is closer to the truth. The décor was cheap, even by Wal-Mart standards. It was quickly apparent that Wal-Mart wasn't spending resources where they did not matter.

The hall was lined, both sides, with little rooms that could double as vendor confessionals, should a vendor feel the urge to confess an episode of high prices to the Wal-Mart buyer boys. About eight by ten, each room contained a folding table, a few folding chairs, and a sign. The narrow entry wall had a single door with the remaining real estate belonging to a glass window. The window and the sign made it clear: There will be no dirty dealing in this hallowed place.

It has been too long for me to recall the sign perfectly, but the message was something like this: "Our goal is to bring quality products to our customers at the lowest price. Our buyers will not accept gratuities of any kind. Any offers of outings, tickets, or merchandise will be refused. If you need to leave a sample of your product, you may arrange to have it shipped back at your expense or it will be donated to charity. If in the course of our negotiations it is appropriate to break for food or drink, our buyers are expected to pay for their own consumption."

I was thirsty but afraid to ask for water! And, I was told, if you did, it came from a vending machine somewhere down that long hall. If you were pitching Wal-Mart, you'd better bring a pocketful of quarters!

Wal-Mart knows who they are and what their customers want, and they are focused like a laser on just that outcome.

Now fly with me further south, where we will visit a powerhouse in the grocery business. The day was hot and we were touring stores in the Atlanta market, talking to employees and looking for ideas in preparation for a proposal to improve customer service. At the third or fourth stop, we entered a brightly lit newer store, cleaner and newer by a long shot than the previous stores.

In the floral department, we introduced ourselves to a middle-aged woman with blonde hair and tired eyes. We told her about our project, asked if she could spare a moment to visit, brought her a soda, and then something totally unexpected happened. At first, she just appeared to have shiny eyes, but in the next instant a tear, then two, fell across her cheeks. Good God! Had we somehow offended this dear woman?

"Ma'am, I am so sorry if we have said something wrong."

She dabbed first one tear and then caught the second in a tissue she fished from a pocket.

"I've worked for this company for 25 years . . . and this is the first time I can remember anybody ever asking for my opinion. And here you are asking me, and wanting to sit with me, bringing a soda and all. I'm sorry," she said.

If you are getting the feeling that we weren't at Wal-Mart anymore, you are right on the money.

The next morning, we were scheduled to meet with the local execs. My client had time on the agenda to present our training plan. I was there for moral support, which I quickly determined would be insufficient. As we stood at the doorway greeting the assembled execs, not one, not a few, but every single one of them asked my client if he had any vendor goodies such as tickets to the Braves, the Hawks, the Falcons, or, failing that, free golf anywhere.

Stay with me.

This same company got the brilliant idea that not only could they profit from sales through consumers, they might even be successful at squeezing their suppliers! As if golf and baseball were not enough, vendors were soon being asked to pay slotting fees, which amount to bribes paid in exchange for being allotted shelf space. Not profits for merchandise sold. Profits for the privilege of simply being allowed to compete!

Here's the quiz:

- Who do you think ultimately paid for the executive goodies?
- Who still believed that corporate ethics had no impact on profitability?

Successful retailers do more than keep an eye on what motivates their customers. Knowing the customer is of little value unless you also know yourself.

4

THE PHYSICAL AND METAPHYSICAL COMPONENTS

Are you a shopper or a buyer? Is the deal almost as important as the product? Do you want to shop alone or at odd hours, like late in the evening or perhaps into the wee hours of the night? Whatever your shopping habits are, we're willing to bet that some of the pet peeves reported by our panelists will ring true for you.

LET'S GET PHYSICAL

If you think customers don't pay much attention to the physical condition of your store, you're wrong. Really wrong. Customers do notice. Sometimes the noticing is conscious, and sometimes it is subliminal, but they always notice . . . every detail.

I think of the many times I have gone shopping with Buns, not to buy or help but just to hang out. Many times she has surprised me by walking past a store I knew would be just her style.

"We don't go in there."

"Why is that?" (I'm playing anthropologist, besides being thrilled with one less store to drag through. I'm figuring that if she tells me why we aren't going in this store, I can notice the same thing about another store and find myself one retail space closer to dinner.)

"They jam so many racks on the floor and so many clothes on a rack that shopping there is more trouble than it's worth."

THE VERBATIMS

It's a bit unusual for online surveys to solicit verbatim comments from respondents. But we did and, for the asking, received just shy of 8,000 of them. The verbatims were promptly fed to the Clusterizer (which you'll meet shortly), and then several sets of human eyeballs made the final analysis.

The inquiry was, "Tell us what you like or do not like about a shopping experience." We received responses of two types. The first type generally started with one of two phrases, either "I like" or "I don't like," followed by a short comment or list. Some were a tad more expressive and began with something to the effect of "I really love it when . . . " or even "I get really hacked off when . . . " Those kinds of comments we figured were fairly equivalent to either "I like" or "I don't like." It's obvious that some of us play the game a bit more intensely.

The second type of verbatim came in the form of a story. These stories revealed more emotion and gave more detail, and we offer them to you without editing.

Here are a few verbatims. These statements reflect respondents' opinions both positive and negative. (As you read on, you'll see more verbatims as they apply throughout.)

+ Aisles wide enough for two carts to pass
+ Organized aisles
− Aisles blocked with stuff being stocked
+ Eye-catching displays
− So many clothes on the rack you can't remove the ones that interest you
+ Advertised specials that are easily found and properly marked
− Unpriced items
− Mispriced items not discovered until you attempt to check out
+ I like unadvertised specials.
− I don't like clothes hung on the wrong rack. I wear women's sizes, and it is very frustrating to pull out something that is a size 3.
− Messy dressing rooms

+ Legitimate sales (Filene's)
+ Multiple dressing rooms and racks for unpurchased clothing (Kohl's)

Pardon Me?

I didn't say anything. That was the window talking. Extrema Products in Ames, Iowa, has developed a way to turn store windows into speakers. The system, called Whispering Windows, involves sticking two puck-sized objects to any window or other flat surface, instantly turning it into audio speakers.

Does it work? An early test at the Peter Jones shop in London resulted in a 40 percent jump in sales the first three weeks!

The Envelope, Please

Ask 8,000 or 9,000 customers who they think does the best job of putting merchandise on display, and they'll tell you in no uncertain terms! We divided the responses into three groups à la good, better, or best, except our groups are more accurately named good, pretty good, and so-awful-it-might-be-part-of-their-strategy.

At first glance, the glamour of retailing seems to rightfully belong to the high-end retailers who cater to the fashionistas, offering $300 shoes and $200 belts. That's the glamour. It's the science that really counts.

Beneath the silks and jewels at Nordstrom, there is science in the form of psychology at work. Should you find yourself shopping for a flat-screen television at Best Buy, you'll discover that merchandising is an art to be practiced anywhere there are customers to buy and product to be sold.

One such Saturday at Best Buy, we were in search of the perfect new television as defined by technology, our budget, and, oh yes, the size of the hole it had to fit in! Got a big hole? Buy a big TV!

Old way: "What size set are you looking for?"

New way: "What size hole do you want to fill?"

Hanging from my Dockers was a 25-foot construction-orange tape measure. We weren't going to need a tape that long, but it doesn't hurt to fantasize. I had the width, height, and depth of our cabinet entered carefully in my phone/PDA and joined the other couples, fathers, and sons measuring tube after tube.

That was when my respect for Best Buy skyrocketed. I noticed a lone shopper writing figures from the little white tag hanging over each set. A price shopper, I thought. But why didn't he just look at the big tag pasted on the front of the set?

I looked closer and there it was—in tiny black and white—the measurements of the set! No need to carry a tape; just read it straight off the tag! (Now, if Best Buy would only notice that the folks over 40 might need the type a whole lot larger, we'd be happier shoppers!)

Too Late?

It's easy to jump on Kmart when they're down, but is there anything that can save Kmart? For certain, it takes money to merchandise in the same style as Nordstrom, Best Buy, and Target, also known as the big dogs, but there is plenty that can be accomplished with a little imagination, a touch of employee training, and a ton of leadership. True, Kmart didn't fare too well with our respondents, but don't give up on them entirely. It wouldn't cost a mint or take very long to turn at least this number around.

Kmart, our respondents say, is close to the bottom of the list. In fact, if you factor out the smaller players and rank only the major players, you also redefine the bottom. Okay, once again, they are down, but are they out?

Be careful! The list in Figure 4.1 is not about which is the best overall retailer. There is no mention of service, price, or selection. The only question we explored was, "Which retailer is best at merchandising the products they sell?"

Notice that Nordstrom ranked number one with an index of 849, while Best Buy, with an index of 454, was second, although not a close second. Also, the number of Nordstrom shoppers was relatively small, which means that a single opinion counts just a bit more than those of the huge number who commented on giant Wal-Mart.

- − I don't like being confused; big stores confuse me.
- + Chain stores that set up all stores the same way, so that no matter which one you shop, you know where to look for things (Wal-Mart)
- + Wal-Mart is the best; they have everything you need there.
- + Happy atmosphere (Target)
- + Stores where I can get everything in one trip

Figure 4.1 *Which retailer is best and which is worst at merchandizing the products they sell.? (For instance, are the products close together, the aisles overflowing, prices clear, etc.?)*

Rank	Retailer	Scorecard
1	Nordstrom	849
2	Best Buy	454
3	Target	381
4	Costco	209
5	Meijer	186
6	Kohl's	165
7	Lowe's	158
8	Wal-Mart	141
9	Sam's Club	135
10	Sears	122
	Walgreens	99
	JCPenney	88
	Home Depot	66
6	Ross	14
5	Family Dollar	14
4	Dollar General	13
3	Kmart	12
2	Big Lots	8
1	Dollar Store	7

Source: BIGresearch, July 2004 (n = 9,232).

– Not sticking to what they are known for; you can't get to the groceries for all the banking services and lawn equipment
+ I can find anything I want at a great price, all from the comfort of home (eBay).
+ Stores that have full-service snack bars
+ Small stores are best for cleanliness, quality products, and friendly service.

OPERATIONAL AWARENESS

You may think that customers don't notice things not related to the hard work of shopping, but they do. They notice when there is extra security; they notice when the register area is understaffed; and they most certainly notice the clerk working checkout. They see; they make mental notes. And maybe not this time or the next or even the next, but eventually, they will act if things aren't right. They cast their economic vote at someone else's place of business.

Check out these comments:

+ Security guards in the parking lot
+ Security guards in the store
− Carousels for checkout instead of cash registers in the departments. Have to wait to check out and only a few clerks in the store. JCPenney has gone to that system, and I dread shopping there.
+ Stations where you can ask for help. Sears has always been very good at this.
+ Easy-to-locate merchandise
− Difficult-to-locate restrooms
− Messy restrooms
− Hunting for shopping carts
− Stores that do not have shopping carts to make it easy to carry your purchases. For the elderly who use them for support or moms with small kids or shoppers with awkward items, they are a necessity.
+ Clean shopping carts
− More stores need electric mobility
− Stores that like to skimp on air-conditioning, or in winter, keep it so warm you have to wear summer clothes to keep from getting sick!
− Employees who think the PA system doesn't work, so they shout
− Stores that do not provide for customers who smoke. I either don't shop or shop online. It may sound silly, but I believe businesses should sell products, not promote a social agenda.
+ Soft music makes me more comfortable and able to relax and take time to look for what I came to buy, and often more.
− When I walk into a store and the music is rap or acid rock, I just turn around.
− Balloons—"I'm allergic to natural rubber. It can kill me!"
+ Stores that smell good
+ A relaxed shopping atmosphere
+ Bright colors
− Long lines
+ Ease of checking out
+ Stores where you can also pay phone, cable, and utility bills

POLICY

Customers do notice your policies, and they become a part of the buying decision. Something as simple as your hours of operation lets customers know if you are running the business for their convenience or for yours.

+ Easy return policies
+ Free shipping and handling
+ Free delivery and setup
+ Layaway service
− Loose dress codes that result in cheap-looking employees
− Dressing rooms that are locked and difficult to find someone to open them
− Extended warranties that mean nothing
+ Being up front about price and warranty and then sticking to promises made
+ I like the way Best Buy sends you off with everything you need to send in for rebates.
+ Bed Bath & Beyond coupons never seem to expire!
+ I like Wal-Mart because they match other store prices.
− I hate it when the cashier hands me my change and the receipt together.
− Refusing to stand behind warranty and leaving you to deal with the manufacturer
− Claiming lowest price plus a percentage off if another retailer has a lower price. It's impossible to compare even when the items are identical, because SKUs are customized to the individual retailer.
+ Honor all coupons, even if they have expired (Steak N Shake)
+ My favorite stores are those that honor competitors' coupons, which can make for one-stop shopping.
− When I went to Meijer to get windshield washer fluid, they had their own brand but not the brand I wanted, so I did not buy fluid that day.
+ Take back unsatisfactory products without hassle, no questions asked (Bed Bath & Beyond)
− Target always asks if I want to open a Target VISA account. This is very annoying every time I go into the store. I already have one!
− Having people check your bags before you leave the store (Wal-Mart and Target)
+ Online shopping for items not carried by the store

+ Special orders for items not normally carried
- Panhandlers in the parking lot
- People in front of the store begging for money for charities
- Starting too early on holidays. What's worse than shopping for Christmas in October? I hate that!
+ Items displayed out of boxes so you can handle them. Wal-Mart and Staples are very good about this.
+ Open 24 hours
+ Stores that have motorized carts for those with disabilities
- Employees smoking in front of the store. It's awful to have to walk through smoke to get to the store. It makes me feel that they don't care for their customers.
+ A greeter (Wal-Mart)
+ Offering soft drinks or coffee while you shop
- Not only do they want the receipt, they want the original packaging. Get real! Am I supposed to rent storage space to keep all the boxes?

PLACES FOR FACES

For the first million or so years of retailing, there was only one way to do business: nose-to-nose. Whether it was the mom-and-pop store at the corner or the traveling salesman stepping respectfully onto your porch, selling was a personal thing. Most buyers knew most sellers personally. In small towns around the world this is still true.

In our hometown of Center Point, Texas, I can count on a hug from Merlyn or Nell when we pick up our laundry at the general store. Kat, at the Burger Barn, doesn't head to our table until she has picked up a small tea, no ice, for Buns and a macho-sized tea for me. While we're eating (you can't call it dining), no doubt we'll see Johnny the local plumber, Butch who owns the feed store, Allen the coach at our small high school, and pretty much anybody who is anybody in our small town.

Center Point is more the exception than the rule and, while there are a few inconveniences, the fact that there is no way to be anonymous guarantees that everyone, even the old farts who rock on the front porch over at the foundry, are going to get good service.

When catalogs arrived on the scene, you could complete your retail transactions from your house, or even the little house behind the house with a cell phone. Now there is the Internet, the harbinger of the paperless and cashless society, which is no longer as useful in the little house.

There is one good thing about the Internet, though; it is the great equalizer. Retailers on the Internet all look the same size. In our office, we have done big business with Internet-based companies that I know are located in the corner of someone's spare bedroom.

To be a player in retail, you have to be everywhere your customers are.

There's no doubt the Internet is still in its infancy. Few have figured how to do more than post a static page on the site and call it a home page. But as bandwidth increases, perhaps our imaginations will follow.

Payless Shoe Source isn't a name that you expect to hear in conversations about innovative uses of technology, but here they are, strutting their stuff on the Web, rolling out an online sweepstakes with a grand prize of a cool $50,000 and, for Payless, an even cooler haul of demographic information.

Visitors to their site are asked about preferences in shoe styles and are invited to play a game based on one of 15 shoe-buying profiles. Players who miss the Grand Prize are likely to win one of the daily prizes: $20 coupons redeemable at, you guessed it, Payless.

In exchange, the company is able to make offers that are custom-tailored to each of the profiles. (What could you do if you had a psychological profile of individual customers?)

+ Small shop owners go that extra yard to make sure you are well treated and served well. (It is worth paying a little extra to keep it in the community and to get good service.)

− Both Lowe's and Home Depot make you type in your zip code when browsing their Web sites, claiming that you are actually browsing the inventory of the store nearest you. Inevitably, when you find what you are looking for, and then go to the bricks-and-mortar store nearest you, it doesn't even carry the item and the service people act like you are from Mars if you mention the Web site said the item was in stock.

− I do most of my shopping on the Internet, and I get disgusted when I have to pay, at the last minute, an additional charge for shipping and handling. Put it in the price!

+ Internet shopping is great; you don't have to put up with people and can take as long as you want. (Great selection and you check out at your leisure)

+ I do most of my shopping online, because I've had enough of rude cashiers.

- When you shop online and are promised overnight delivery and it actually comes a day later . . . and there is always an excuse (Amazon)
- I spend as little time as possible in stores and spend less money that way.
+ If you have been to a store a number of times and the salespeople get to know you, that is wonderful. When you come into the store, they greet you by name and say, "Something came in I think might interest you."
+ Jack's, an old-fashioned and independent hardware store, always has what I need and knows where it is. Jack and his wife are extremely knowledgeable. They don't like kids in their store either!
+ People who remember my name. We live in a small town, and it shouldn't be hard to do.

TALK TO ME

If listening is part of selling—and it is—then live chat via the Internet may be the next hot idea. Credit unions and banks have been doing it for years, and online retailers were quick to follow. Customers log on, browse to their heart's content, and, when ready, click for a bit of company.

I've seen it in action at Lands' End and again at Affinity Fedeal Credit Union.

Affinity

Talk's not cheap, or is it? On the same day that American Airlines announced a nonrefundable fee for talking to a live AA agent (September, 2004), I talked to Affinity Federal Credit Union in Basking Ridge, New Jersey, where talk is still cheap. In fact, it's free!

In late 2001, Affinity, whose field of membership includes high-tech giants AT&T and Lucent, was looking for a way to personalize the online experience. Live chat seemed like a natural. The idea is simple—offer visitors to your site an opportunity to interact directly with customer service representatives in the form of a two-way, on-screen chat.

The secure version lies behind the firewall of the home banking platform, which allows member relations specialists to deal with any level of financial information secure in the identity of the visitor. Member relations specialists, who call themselves chat experts, are truly experts.

They are selected from the pool of veteran members of the member relations department and are screened for their writing and grammar skills, as well as their ability to multitask.

It takes a competent, confident organization to offer online chat service. Everything a chat expert says to a customer leaves a data trail. It's in writing, so to speak, and grammar errors stick out like a sore thumb. To further complicate matters, chat experts routinely juggle three chats simultaneously! Add in the fact that many of Affinity's customers (who are called members) are also multitasking, and member relations specialists have to be very careful about which information they send!

Fortunately, many of the responses to FAQs are canned, although they can be personalized to specifically address the member online. Affinity members have been known to be on live chat at the same time they are e-mailing another department and waiting for still another Affinity department to pick up the phone!

Surprisingly, some chat does not start with the intention to chat. A member may be working online and have a question about his or her account or how to navigate the site. One click on the live chat icon and members are instantly connected to a chat expert. A nonmember may visit the nonsecure site and "chat in" for more information. Either way, the average chat will last eight to nine minutes.

But the question remains, "Is free talk really cheap talk?" Well, if not cheap, this talk is at least cheaper. Chat experts were drawn from the Call Center, where CSRs (customer service representatives) still handle calls the old-fashioned way—one at a time. Chat experts are working three calls at a time. Better yet, when members indicate they wish to close their accounts, the chat experts have an incredible 60 percent save rate! And because chat experts meet members in such a nonthreatening environment, cross-selling and the resultant product penetration are at an all-time high.

Affinity officials say their members love it! It's quick, it's easy, and it fits their lifestyle, because they can use it at home or at work. In fact, in nearly four years, there have been zero complaints, many unsolicited testimonials, and the original staff remains unchanged! This is one time when customers talk, you can, too!

WHY WE BUY

Human emotion is an influence on why we buy. We buy out of happiness when shopping for the new baby. We buy out of fear when we purchase a handgun or an alarm system. We can buy out of anger or spite, love or sentimentality, but basically we buy for one of only two reasons:

1. We think the purchase will make us feel good (or at least better).
2. We are afraid of feeling bad because we did not buy.

Feel good or feel bad or perhaps a combination of the two, but any way you slice it, that's why we buy.

Recently, when I spoke to the folks at SUNY in Cortland, New York, I asked the chief of retail operations what was hot on college campuses this year. Without hesitation, she rattled off, "Thongs, micro-mini skirts, and . . . " I was so taken aback, my hearing shutdown before she got to item number three. Call me old–fashioned, but it's been a long time since the '60s.

When our kiddo was a teenager, his favorite shoes were a pair of black-and-white-checked Van's canvas shoes. All he was missing was the red nose and Ringling Brothers would have come calling. Why? Because that's what everyone else was wearing and he would feel bad to not fit in.

Hanging in my closet is the "ice cream" suit. I'm waiting for it to come back in style, because I imagine I look dashing in it. That suit makes me feel good, but I'm not wearing it to Sporty's tonight. I doubt there will be any other men wearing a near-polyester, almost-white suit, and that would make me feel bad.

What makes us feel good about ourselves one day may have the opposite or no effect at all the next.

For example, *Chief Marketer* (December, 2003) reported that 57 percent of consumers say they don't care if a product was made in the USA. That's a long way from the days in the not-too-distant past when retailers made a big to-do over products made in the USA. Do you remember the commercial with all the people singing "Look for the union label"? History. "Made in the USA" made us feel good. "Cheap" seems to make us feel better. (By the way, the "Made in the USA" sentiment is much stronger among older consumers.)

What makes you feel good, and would you pay extra to get it?

In the past week (August, 2004), we heard an apology from the CEO of Delta Airlines for a survey question that asked Delta customers if they would be willing to pay extra to know that their calls to reservations were answered by Americans rather than East Indians. That's not exactly what you would call PC (politically correct), and the Delta chief was quick to respond. What's your guess? Would a "Made in the USA" phone experience be worth an extra $5 or $10? Or do you think it really matters?

No matter what your answer, you can't and won't know what people will buy and pay for until you get customers to talk.

+ Friendly people make all the difference to me. People who smile and make small talk make you feel good. Applebee's in my town is great for this; they like to have fun at their jobs.
+ When someone treats you like you are the only person in the place. Ruby Tuesday is a wonderful place for great service.
– When they hurry you to make a decision
+ I love it when the clerk takes time to suggest items for me to try on and keeps them coming while I am in the dressing room. (McRae's, Dillard's, The Dress Barn)
– Women's clothing stores where they tell you everything you try on looks good, even when it doesn't
+ I like smaller stores where they are likely to be more interested in helping you. (Victoria's Secret)
+ Free advice from well-informed, smiling employees who have the eagerness to find the answers if they don't know them. Bry-an's Computers really shines when it comes to these things!
– Dealing with people who cannot speak English
+ They remember your name, even if the computer tells them you shop there all the time.
+ Food sampling at Sam's Club. It's always such a treat, and you get to try some new things without having to buy them first and keep the kids happy, too!
+ Having Starbucks or other gourmet coffee in the store and being allowed to drink while you are shopping
– Disrespectful cashiers who think you are wasting their time or making them work, especially teenagers who have a manager who is just as bad
+ I like it when someone recognizes that I do a lot of business with the company.
+ When supermarket staff asks if you need help to your vehicle. Safeway—now that's what I call old-fashioned courtesy.
+ Small family-owned restaurants are best for service and appreciation for your business.
– Cell phone people who just want your money and don't want to explain how the phone works

- Checkout clerks who don't wait until you put your money away before moving on to the next customer
- When you buy new clothes and the clerk just rolls them up and stuffs them into a bag
+ I find the most pleasant cashiers where I shop the most. (Kmart and Giant Eagle)
- I won't shop at a store that has an overwhelming aroma caused by candles or sprays.
- I hate the freezer aisles because they are so cold.
- Impatient fast-food order-takers
- Incorrect fast-food orders
+ Bookstore café to sit and read and drink coffee. It's a nice break from everyday drudgery. (Barnes & Noble)
+ When businesses spot their mistakes before you do (Pizza Hut)
+ Having what I need every time (Lowe's, Wal-Mart, and Staples)
- We live in a global economy, but the influx of goods not made in this country is appalling. Wal-Mart and Hewlett-Packard are two offenders that really get to me. Wal-Mart is responsible for 12 percent of the trade deficit with China. Labels don't always say clearly where a product is made. As for HP, I recently purchased a new printer and had problems getting it to work with my system. I was shocked that the customer service rep who answered my call was in India.

THE INSIDE SCOOP

An article from the "Inside Business" section of *Time* asks, "Is your coffee unfair?" The gist of the article is that much of the coffee consumed in the United States is purchased at a price lower than the cost of production. Free marketers argue that demand (i.e., price) is the surest way to keep supply at the right level, while others, crying foul, insist that fair trade should also embrace the idea of trading fairly. Third world family farmers, they say, deserve to be paid a living wage for coffee beans and other products sold to countries able, by far, to pay a price that will allow the farmers to survive, if not prosper.

Last year, only $208 million of a total world market of $19.2 billion in coffee beans were sold with Fair Trade certification. However, a number of large users are poised to jump on the bandwagon, partly because they can market under the Fair Trade banner and tell the story behind each product. This attempt to humanize a product that is usually sold as a commodity adds value and allows Fair Trade products to be sold at a premium.

Will your customers pay more? You won't know for sure until your customers talk.

WHO DECIDES?

Who is the decision maker for your product? For McDonald's on a Saturday morning, I'm betting it's a four-year-old in search of a Happy Meal. For Mickey D's at 6 AM on a Monday morning, my money is on the construction worker looking for a quick breakfast.

The decision maker in the family changes, according to product, cost, age, even time of day.

For years, auto dealers lost sales by ignoring women. We know of one woman who was actually told, "When you get serious about buying a car, bring your husband back with you." Fred Vang, automotive consultant in Santa Fe, New Mexico, likes to tell of the time while working in a BMW dealership that the salesperson who was up next let Fred take his place. He had seen a car full of Filipino men pull onto the sales drive. They were slight, brown, and carried what looked to be purses.

Fred happily took them on as prospective clients. He asked about their country. He inquired about their food preferences and then called home to Martha to ask how she felt about unexpected company for dinner. Was Fred rewarded for listening? Over the course of the next few years, Fred sold this group and their family members a grand total of 18 new cars!

When customers talk, be prepared to listen.

Women are talking on the Internet. The medium that many assumed would be the haunt for nerds and geeks has, as of last year, been dominated by women. Girls go online earlier than boys, have more influence over family purchase decisions, and, once connected, are more active than boys.

When customers talk, it helps to know who they are!

Back up to the paragraph about Fred and the 18 cars sold. We might want to add another moral to that story: If you want customers to talk, you may have to start the conversation.

- A female alone not getting any attention
- Car dealerships that judge people on looks alone and will not help younger customers
- Being overweight and hardly ever approached and waited on. When I weighed 170 pounds more, I was usually not the clerk's first priority and preferred to get in and get out as fast as possible.
- Car salespersons who seem to have the attitude that women can't choose a car or must wait until their husbands can come along
- Mechanics who take advantage of women. There should be a law against this.

BUILDING SHARE OF CUSTOMER

The King of Customer Share is Wal-Mart. When we ask consumers where they shop most for women's clothes, prescription drugs, and a handful of other categories, Wal-Mart is the name that keeps rising to the surface. Wal-Mart does more than offer many categories, they also keep customers in the store long enough to actually buy them.

How do they do it? Price, selection, and value are good for a start. For example, when it comes to women's clothing, 48 percent of women who buy their clothing at Wal-Mart also buy shoes there. In comparison, only 23.6 percent of Macy's customers, 23.5 percent of Sears, 22.7 percent of JCPenney, and 22 percent of Target customers say the same. In approximate terms, we could say that Wal-Mart crosses over customers at double the rate of its competitors.

The story is much the same for prescription drugs, where 83 percent of the folks who say they shop Wal-Mart most often for prescription drugs also purchase their health and beauty aids from the giant retailer. The national retailer who comes closest to matching their rate, which isn't close at all, is CVS with what now looks like a paltry 41.4 percent crossover.

How important is share of customer? In a competitive retail market, retailers' choices for growth are usually limited to selling more to current customers or stealing customers from the competition. Wal-Mart has been able to excel at both. "In order to become the biggest, you have to be able to steal customers from competitors, and Wal-Mart has done a great job of this," said Gary Drenik of BIGresearch. "However, in order to stay big, you've got to get an ever-increasing share of customer expenditures, and Wal-Mart does this better than anyone."

FIGURE 4.2 *Customer Share at Wal-Mart versus Kohl's by Income Level*

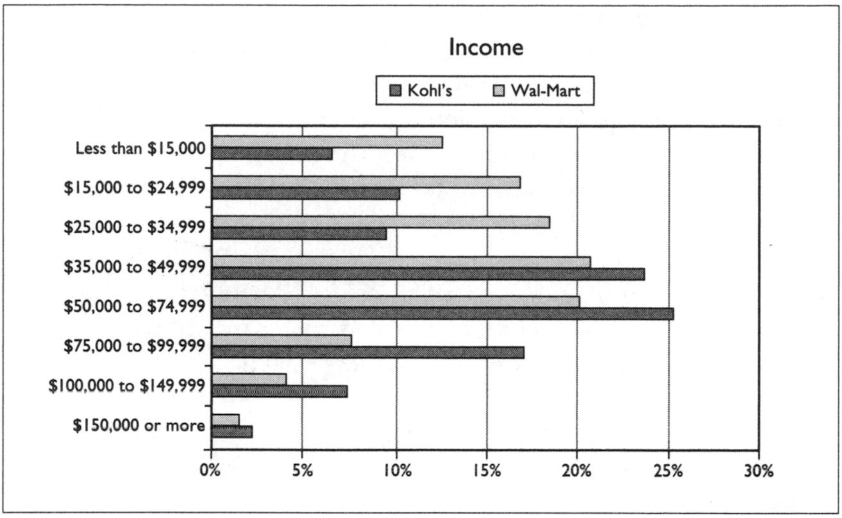

Source: BIGresearch, July 2004 (n = 9,232).

Part of the Wal-Mart success story is due to the fact that anyone can be a Wal-Mart customer, but not everyone can shop at higher-priced retailers. (See Figure 4.2.) A sample of Wal-Mart customers will look like they were lifted from a meeting of the United Nations, where poor nations and rich nations each have voting rights.

STEAL YOUR OWN CUSTOMERS!

If the customers you already have were encouraged to come in twice as often, or purchase twice as much, you could double your sales without having to attract a single new customer. Skip the TV commercials. Dump the newspaper insert. Sell twice as much to the ones you've got by getting them to cross over to other departments!

Begin by discovering what your current crossover rates for various categories are. You'll also want to know the crossover rates of your competition. You don't really need to know this, but it will serve as a benchmark of sorts. And don't allow the competition to set the bar too low!

The next step is to find out the reasons why your customers choose you for the categories you have targeted. Do the same for your competitors. Be sure to ask your current customers why they do not shop you most often in other categories.

Now you are ready to make a plan. Decide if you want to go head-to-head with the competition, or if you would rather zig when the other guy zags. For example, competing with Wal-Mart on price might be self-defeating. If there is a large enough potential market, you may be better off competing on quality, selection, or service.

The contrarian approach is often the winning approach. While American Airlines was piling on food service and routing both planes and passengers through hub cities, little ole Southwest Airlines was serving peanuts and cold beer and flying point-to-point. While the other airlines were adding mission-specific aircraft to their fleets, Southwest stuck with one type of aircraft and created routes that fit the plane.

Guess who is the most profitable? Guess what little puppy is now the big dog?

In the fast-food restaurant segment, we have watched a seemingly unstoppable McDonald's face rather stiff competition from small regional operators that decided they could serve a burger as fast, if not faster than the arched competitor. Rather than compete with Mickey D's on price, the other guys focused on selection and dethroned Burger King "when it comes to having it your way."

But you can't create a game plan without first listening to customers and discovering why they buy. P.S.: Your opinion doesn't count!

+ JCPenney offers more personal service than anyone, AND there are people to help who seem to know what they are talking about!
+ I like shopping at a department store where I get personal service to coordinate my purchases and where I get honest opinions.
− Why are items that are naturally purchased together located in different departments?
+ One-stop shopping (Wal-Mart)
+ Someone who will call other stores in the area to help find what you want
− Clerks who don't care if you buy. Any retailer who hires young kids as clerks is looking for trouble.
− Clerks who point in a general direction and whine, "If we have it, it will be over there."
+ I like to be pointed in the right direction and then left alone to shop.
+ Asking for assistance and having the employee actually taking me to the item rather than telling me the aisle number and pointing (Office Max)

+ Salespersons willing to help you, even if they have to leave their area to do so
+ I call the manager when I get great service, hoping to make a positive example of the employee.
+ Salespersons who come up and ask, "May I help you?" and then do just that: no sales pitches, just help. Wal-Mart in our area has this type of retail people.
− Cashiers who are either so lazy or tired they move at a snail's pace; my time is valuable also. Kmart is the biggest offender. Between my discretionary spending and groceries for my family, Kmart is losing $400 to $500 per month. I know it's not much to a large chain, but I certainly can't be the only one who feels this way. Target gets all my discretionary spending now.

The difference between the amateur and the pro lies in the details. Every retailer sells product, every restaurateur serves food. So it's not the big stuff. It's the little stuff. And nothing escapes the eagle eyes of the customers. They see, they record, and they talk.

5

HOW TO LISTEN
TO YOUR CUSTOMERS

The universal truth is that customers want to be respected. Disrespect their time by making them wait unnecessarily, and you have committed an unforgivable personal affront. Disrespect their intelligence by making hokey offers, and boy, the game is on. Disrespect a customer by offering shoddy service or product, and you are left only with price on which to deal.

On the other hand, give the customer a little status, and you are on your way to a profitable relationship.

One of the best ways to show respect for your customers is to let them know that they have the attention of the boss, el Hefe, the Big Cheese. Everyone likes to be able to say, "I know the owner and the owner knows me." Or to put it in borrowed words, "I'd rather meet a dumb owner than a sharp manager."

EVERY CUSTOMER IS A
CANDIDATE FOR RESPECT

One customer group that is dying for respect is the young adult group. Young working adults are very aware of their spending power, and, because this group is most likely to be just starting out in the adult economy, they want respect for their hard-earned, they-didn't-come-from-daddy dollars.

A few weeks after Sporty's opened, we were discovered by the camp counselors who ride herd over the small army of summer campers that invades our quiet river valley every June. One night a week, the counselors slip away from their charges and head into town for a little R & R. One evening, we had the NBA play-offs on all 18 televisions at Sporty's, and, in the words of the hostess on duty, "the place was rockin'." It was a nice surprise to watch a group of 6 early-arriving counselors grow to become a long table of 25 that stretched clear across our largest dining room. They were laughing and teasing and, in general, just having a good time sipping from frosted mugs, when "the old people" approached one end of the snaking train of tables.

"Excuse me, folks!" My voice had the effect of holding up two fingers at a Cub Scout banquet. You should have seen the looks on their faces. I understood in a heartbeat what they expected me to say, especially after I introduced myself as one of the owners. What they thought I was about to say was: "You need to keep it down. We have other customers who want to eat without being disturbed. Also, don't ask for separate checks. And, in case you haven't noticed, it is our policy to add an 18 percent gratuity for large parties."

Instead, they heard this: "Sorry to interrupt your good time, but we just wanted to say thank you for coming to Sporty's tonight. We want you to have fun and enjoy yourself. You deserve a break, and we're glad you chose us tonight. If there's anything that you want, just ask and we'll do our best to accommodate. We're heading to the house now, but we wanted to say hello first and remind you that our telephone number is right on the menu if you should need us. (Try not to need us!) Have fun, be safe, and we'll see you next time! We appreciate your business."

As we walked away from the group, we overheard a male voice say, "Wow, that was nice!" followed by an obviously surprised female voice saying, "That was amazing!"

With 18 televisions, there are times when it would be possible for every seated table to have its choice of programming. At most sports-themed operations, the televisions are strictly hands-off. At Sporty's, you are likely to hear: "Are you watching what you wanted to watch? If you're not, we can bring you a remote and you can watch whatever turns you on, except for Jerry Springer!"

We are often met with a surprised look and a "No, thanks." So we follow up with, "Hey, this is America. You're at Sporty's. Do what you want!" Isn't it a sad commentary that you can amaze customers with something as pedestrian as respect?

The most respectful thing you can do for a customer is to listen and at the very least give consideration to their requests.

At Sporty's, we leave a guest comment card with each guest check. Every card that is negative and every card that offers a suggestion get a personal response from me. (This may be impossible to sustain, because the same applies to each of my reader comments.) This week, we have had requests for fresh salmon, baked eggplant, and a host of menu items that sound great but do not fit our concept. We also had a suggestion to add a vegetarian burger, which we're taste-testing, along with an idea to create a smaller version of our Big Dog dessert, to be called a Little Puppy.

Neither of those potentially good ideas would have come our way had we not had in place a formal system for getting in front of the customer. And we have lost count of the number of times our guests have said, "Thanks for taking time to talk with us!"

Too bad that when it comes to listening to customers the playing field is so un-level. The big players have their MIS departments, their market research departments, and their gurus of finance and economics. It's too bad the owner of the local dry cleaner can run rings around them all, simply by leaning across the counter. "Hey! Good to see you again! Are those plastic retainers we've been putting on your collars helping keep their shape? Just out of curiosity, why exactly do you choose us as your dry cleaner? Got any suggestions as to how we might do an even better job?"

Keep in mind that listening is the best way to discover what is on your customers' minds, what problems they have that you might solve, or where else they may be shopping and why.

HOW TO LISTEN

Saying that you want to listen to your customers is a nice first step, but not enough. All communications have two ends, sender and receiver. And unless the sender sends, it wouldn't matter if the receiver had ears the size of Frisbees.

Here's what has to happen:

1. Listen to the right voice.
2. Be a trusted listener.
3. Ask the right questions.

4. Make the correct interpretation.
5. Take action.

LISTEN TO THE RIGHT VOICE . . .

. . . by asking the right customer.

In a business sense, not all customers are equal. The elderly shopper who only buys on deal may be a lovely person but cannot be considered equal to the impulse buyer with unlimited resources.

On hearing that we do not have a full-service bar at Sporty's, a lady replied, "Well, if I can't get a good mixed drink, I'll have to go someplace else." As she was walking out the door, one of our servers said, "Maybe we should apply for a liquor license." Maybe, maybe not. The fact is, we're a casual café not a cocktail lounge. That's not our concept, and the lady just won't be our customer. Sometimes, you must say, "Great idea, but that's not my customer." At Sporty's, we serve comfort food in large portions. I enjoy fine dining as much as the next guy, but Sporty's isn't fine dining. If you need a lobster fix, we aren't the place.

Asking the wrong customer the right question will always yield a useless, perhaps misleading response.

And who is the right customer? The right customer is someone who has the potential for being highly profitable. Anyone not in that group should be respected but not catered to. (You may be surprised to discover that customers you think are profitable, may not be, so look carefully.)

An automobile manufacturer approached BIGresearch with a problem. It had run a huge promotional campaign to encourage new car buyers to test-drive their latest minivan. Unfortunately, the company threw a wonderful party, but nobody came. Disappointed and a bit red-faced, the executives in charge of the fiasco wanted to find out why the miserable turnout had produced even more miserable sales. "Find out why so few people actually purchased as a result of the test-drive," was the order directed by the car company.

Not a bad question, unless it's the only question. The other questions should have discovered the profile of the folks who actually responded to the campaign: whether they purchased another vehicle, why they eliminated the client's new vehicle, and a dozen others along that same line.

But the payoff questions were those posed to consumers who did not respond to the offer but nonetheless were in the market for a new automobile. The data pay dirt lies in questions such as: "Did you know about the campaign?" "What would have motivated you to go for a test drive?" "What do you already know about the vehicle?" "Why did you eliminate it as a potential new vehicle for you?" Those questions have meat. They will yield actionable information that will lead to trial and sales.

Always Follow Up

Almost any survey question you could ask will generate a follow-up question. Fail to ask the follow-up question, and you risk missing key data.

> Question: "How important is style in your decision when purchasing shoes?"
> Follow-up: "How do you determine what the latest fashion is?"
> Follow-up: "How much do you expect a stylish pair of shoes to cost?"
> Follow-up: "How often do you pay that amount for shoes?"

You could go on forever. Follow up until you have the data narrow enough to act on it.

BE A TRUSTED LISTENER

When communication has a negative consequence, or is thought to be of no consequence, it stops.

Sitting in an airport departure lounge, I was appalled to hear the following communication between a woman identified as Mommy (probably an alias) and a two-year-old named Jason.

"Jason, Mommy said no."

Jason responded, but not verbally. He continued to run along the crowded hallway.

"Jason! I'm not going to tell you one more time!" Mommy didn't move, and Jason continued a drunken imitation of a tornado that nearly bowled over a businessman with a cell phone glued to his ear.

"Alright, mister! Mommy's going to count to three. One. Two," followed by a dejected, "Three," followed by a rolling of the eyes and the sad disclaimer, "I don't know why he won't listen."

We could write a book on the communication between Jason and Mommy, but suffice it to say that for Jason there were no consequences to the exchange, which pretty much rendered it useless. Communication with negative consequences, real or imagined, doesn't stop. It never gets started. People are only likely to communicate if they believe that the consequences will be good. And "good" is defined by the communicator, not the listener.

If the communicator believes nothing will happen, or worse that the consequences will be negative, communication will not occur. This is as true for internal customers as it is for paying customers. Give me a little positive feedback this time, or there darned well won't be a next time. This explains why so few of your customers complain—to you. And an eager audience explains why unhappy customers find it so easy to tell their friends!

What are the consequences for communicating with you?

- Nothing makes me angrier than when I find a better deal, switch or cancel my existing service, and then am offered a cheaper rate just to get my business back. Why should I have to cancel my service in order to be offered a better deal?
- When they promise a delivery time and then don't show up (Sears)
- I had two five-year-olds missing in the store for over an hour. We asked in the first 20 minutes for the police to be called, and the manager said he had called them. Thirty minutes later, no police and still no girls. Only one worker helped us search for our children. We went nuts looking for them! I wondered how the girls could have disappeared so quickly and decided to check the stock area nearest where we had been standing when they vanished. I saw movement and there were our girls after an hour and 20 minutes of frantic searching. I called the police to ask why they hadn't responded and was told there was no record of a call. The excuse given by the store was that the store manager could not leave his office, because he was counting money!
- Service companies such as Verizon, Gateway, Sears, the U.S. Postal Service, and any company that cares about customers should have a real human being answering the initial call. Then I can understand being routed to a menu of options. But to call up a company and endure four or five or a dozen rings (a phone company, for example, should be able to afford multiple lines) to

hit a mechanical voice, offering a few cold, sometimes confusing choices.

- Being often utterly unable to speak to a person is the single worst offense against the American consumer. How expensive can it be to hire a $7 an hour employee to spend ten seconds routing customers to the right department? I'm not asking for service at this point, but at least allow me the illusion that I can actually talk to somebody!

- I will never again purchase a gift card at Best Buy. During the holidays, I gave each of my grandsons (six) a $50 gift card at Best Buy. One of the little boys lost his card, but I had the receipt with the number of the missing card. I gave this to my daughter to take to the store. After waiting 45 minutes on the customer service line, she was told that only corporate could help us. After many phone calls, we spoke to someone and were advised it would take eight weeks to receive the new card. It actually took three months. I wrote an e-mail explaining our displeasure and reminding them that our family spends over $3,000 each year in gift cards. I never received a response. That is unacceptable, and Best Buy will not be selling any more gift cards to members of my family.

- I dislike the $9.99 tactic. Why not just make it $10? And I really don't understand the $1.69.9 for gasoline. Let's keep it as simple as possible please.

- Faking the biggest sale of the year just before they do a seasonal clearance

Bombardier Listens

It has low wings swept rearward at such an angle that it looks fast just sitting on the ramp. Two whisper-quiet engines mounted high on the tail set the standard in low-noise super-midsize corporate airliners. You may not hear it when it flies over your neighborhood, but the Bombardier Challenger 300 business jet is a monument to corporate listening.

You might think that since Bombardier manufactures the regional jets that brought commercial jet service to many small and midsize markets that building the Challenger 300 would be a simple matter of downsizing a regional jet. But Bombardier didn't take the easy way out. Instead, they recognized that the customer for a regional jet is entirely different from a corporate buyer. Starting from a blank page, Bombardier began developing the 300 by finding out what the customer wanted.

They surveyed the corporate market in 1996, revalidated the research in 1997, and continued asking customers throughout the process.

Customers asked for a jet with a standup cabin, transcontinental range for eight passengers, and able to fly into airports with only modest-length runways.

Pilots and owners were included on all the big decisions and many of the small ones, too. They participated in engine selection (a large detail) and made suggestions about switch and instrument placement (small details). Honeywell, the supplier of the jet engines, also caught the spirit and employed advisory panels of business jet owners and pilots. These panels asked for engines with low parts counts and almost unlimited access for maintenance without having to remove the engines from the plane.

But here's the big question. Now that the plane is available, is anyone actually buying? Bombardier quickly took orders for the first 100 Challenger 300s, proving conclusively that customers will buy what they ask for.

But you have to ask!

Getting in Front of the Customer

Sometimes, the best approach is the direct approach, and a few smart operators have decided that organizing a customer council is one sure way to get customer buy-in.

Southwest Airlines is known for inviting frequent flyers to assist in the hiring of new flight attendants. The idea is simple: Customers will have more interaction with flight attendants than supervisors, so why not let them have a say in the hiring decision.

Many franchise organizations have franchise advisory boards consisting of sometimes-elected representatives from the franchise community. These boards, or councils, are often given approval authority over marketing budgets, introductions of new products, even substantive policy decisions that directly impact the organization. As an aside, think about the buy-in that comes when people have a say in the decisions that impact their lives and livelihoods.

Saturn was built on the principle of customer involvement. Owners of Saturn automobiles are invited to watch their car be built via the Internet. Dealerships invite owners to return for maintenance seminars, barbeques, and other owner-involving events. Getting in front of the Saturn customer has created a cultlike aura around ownership. You don't just drive a Saturn, you experience one.

Chevrolet built one of the all-time ugliest vehicles on the planet, the Avalanche. But rather than admit their mistake, they organized it. Now Avalanche owners, often with the help of local dealers, can join an Avalanche truck club, which acts, I'm just guessing here, as a support group for buyers with poor taste.

The point is this: Get in front of your customers. Organize before they do. Listening doesn't have to happen only under formal conditions. You can learn a lot just by asking, and any event should be considered a listening opportunity.

Compute This!

Here's evidence that trust comes from action.

In the fall of 2003, *Computerworld*, the magazine for the information technology crowd, published an article on ComputerWorld.com that turned out to be a hoax. They could have pulled the article from the Web site, published a retraction somewhere inconspicuous, or ignored it entirely in the hope that no one would notice.

They could have, but they didn't.

Editor-in-chief Maryfran Johnson responded with a full Monty, which included a follow-up story detailing what happened. And what was the impact on readers? Positive! Readers now have tangible proof that the editors of *Computerworld* are trustworthy. They know that even if something is not correct as originally published, it will be right thanks to the integrity of the staff.

To advertisers, the whole affair only served to demonstrate that their advertising messages were appearing in a highly credible, highly respected industry environment.

You're Not Listening to Me

Listening is a skill you learn. It may be "only human," but too many clerks and companies are so busy sending out messages that very little communication filters in. If we were as good at listening as we are at marketing, the market would tell us exactly what we need to do to succeed.

At the heart of poor listening, you will find incompetence. Incompetent organizations and performers know that they are incompetent. They attempt to hide their incompetence under a torrent of outbound communication, while at the same time blocking any inbound communication that might reveal their shortcomings. "It's not my job," is not the response of a lazy person. It is the theme song of the incompetent.

While building our new restaurant, I had the dubious honor of having the following conversations in back-to-back phone calls, first to a local sign company:

> "Hi, my name is Scott, and I'm looking for a traffic sign that has the icon of a bicycle. Do you have them in stock and, if you do, how much and what size are they?"
> "You have to talk to Shirley."
> "OK, may I speak with Shirley?"
> "She's in a meeting."
> "Could you just tell me if you have the sign I am looking for?"
> "That would be up to Shirley."

The second conversation was with a restaurant supply house:

> "Hello?"
> "Is this XX Restaurant Supply?"
> "Yes."
> "I'm sorry, I was a thrown off a little when you answered by just saying hello."
> "Well, we aren't open."
> "Oh, I get it. You aren't XX Restaurant Supply until you open."
> "Sorta."
> "Well, this is Scott from Sporty's, and I was wondering where my dining room furniture is. Remember, I called yesterday, talked to you and Rocky, and was told that someone would call me right back. No one ever called."
> "Rocky went home sick."
> "It would have been alright for you to have called me and told me that."
> "That would have been up to Rocky."

Listening for Fun and Profit

Listening is about a whole lot more than fixing problems. Smart operators can actively involve their customers in such forward-thinking projects as product development. Staples, the office supply people, offered a $25,000 prize to customers who came up with a new product idea that the company could choose to market.

Did they have a winner? You bet! A panel of judges and more than 147,000 online votes declared Wordlock, a combination lock that uses easy-to-remember words instead of number sequences, the winning idea. Amateur inventor Todd Basche created the idea that was deemed best of the 8,000-plus invention ideas submitted. (If you want to know, nearly 1,100 of those ideas involved writing instruments; 900 involved clips, staples, or adhesives; and 181 brainstorms involved the common envelope!)

The real beauty of the process was how it involved real customers, talking in a forum that invited them to tell what problems needed to be solved, and then telling the retailer exactly how to solve them.

Truly, the customer is the first outside expert who needs to be hired.

Grace Performance Chemicals understands that nobody knows their products quite as well as their customers. So Grace decided to ask! Actually, the directive was to observe. Sales reps for the company that makes chemical supplies and materials for the construction and packaging industries were told to look for innovative and unexpected ways that customers put Grace products to work. Boy, were they surprised!

Grace waterproofing materials were being used to soundproof automobiles, patch tents, and repair boots! Not that the company endorsed such off-the-wall applications, but the search for new ideas turned into 134 anecdotes that eventually became seven compelling ideas with a sales potential in the millions.

Grace named their campaign "Customers Do the Darnedest Things," and it's a killer example of what you can learn when customers talk, and you listen!

Happy Listening

Some companies do the right thing because it's the right thing. Some companies do the right thing because it's also the smart thing. As I was about to write this short piece on corporate ethics and corporate listening, an e-zine that I subscribe to fell into my electronic in basket. The headline read: "McDonald's Enhances Happy Meals Worldwide." Why do you suppose the good folks under the arches would mess with a product that has been a runaway success for two and a half decades? Because they listened to their customers!

Among what McDonald's calls "menu enhancements" are 1% milk in the United States, fruit cups in Italy, bottled water and low-fat yogurt in Spain, cereal bars in Romania, and organic milk in the UK. The new Happy Meal graphics feature children playing sports and having fun with friends.

Do you suppose this could have anything to do with the recent announcement that obesity is the second leading cause of death in the United States? A quick search of the Internet yielded more than 34,000 references to cheeseburgers! The U.S. House of Representatives passed a bill authored by a Florida congressman that protects purveyors of fatty foods from lawsuits claiming they were complacent in obesity. On our menu at Sporty's, we have covered ourselves with this warning: "If you eat too much of our food and sit on your butt . . . it will get big!"

Also, in 12-point type, our menu announces: "Our kitchen will always be immaculate. You can ask to see it. Our service will always be fast and friendly. You can feel comfortable asking to see one of our managers. If you are not happy for any reason, you can call Scott. His cell phone number is . . . . If you're not happy, we're not happy."

In another life, we owned a fast-food restaurant where we had our home phone posted right on the menu board. In eight years, we had exactly two customers call us at home. The first was so shocked that it was actually our home phone number that he apologized and hung up before ever voicing a complaint. The second call came three weeks after we had sold the restaurant!

At three months into our new restaurant, I have had three calls, exactly three more than I expected. The first came in week one while I was changing planes in Phoenix. (Yes, I was out of town on business the first week we were open. You can do that if you have a great management team, and ours is the best!)

"Hello! Pants phone!" (I may not be in the office when you call, but chances are if I'm accepting calls I am wearing my pants. So call my office or call my pants phone—either way you're in for an experience!) I shouted my answer as I stepped timidly down the stairs of a regional jet, "Sorry, I can't hear you. I'll call you right back."

"This is Scott. You just called?"

"Yes. This is Jay Sanchez. I was in your restaurant at lunch." Swell, a complaint already, I thought.

"Yes, sir! How can I help?"

"I have to tell you the food was great." Okay, it's going to be a service issue, not something I expected.

"And?" I prompted, not really wanting to hear the gory details.

"Oh, the service was terrific! You've hired a lot of smiling people." Now, I'm totally lost. It's not the food. It's not the service. Maybe he's a vendor. "I have just one question about the floor." Oh, no, he must have slipped and injured himself.

"Yes, sir?"

"Is that real wood or is it vinyl?"

Whew! Thankfully, the other two were just as innocuous. The point is simple. If you ask, you had better be prepared to listen! There is an unexpected side benefit to listening to your customers. If your employees know that customers can comfortably talk to the boss, they are a tad more likely to give them something positive to talk about!

ASK THE RIGHT QUESTIONS

I am writing from a megasized hotel room in Nashville, where its operators are known as the best in the business. As luck would have it, we have speaking engagements in three of their company properties this week. So it is interesting to see if they are a learning corporation or stuck on one idea (albeit a very good one).

If you imagined me sitting at the desk in my hotel room quietly tapping away while Buns burns through yet another mystery novel, you would be half right. Buns is reading one of her omnipresent paperbacks, and I am in one corner, quietly attending to the writing business. But I am not sitting at the desk, because, as usual, the hotel room desks are ordered by a designer who thinks long and hard about the fabric on the chair but not one iota about how the chair will actually be used.

I'm a fairly tall guy, but darned if I don't start singing à la Carlos Santana every time I sit at a hotel room desk: "All my friends write a little lower. Low writers, write a little slower." (A good play on words, don't you think?)

Desk chairs in hotels are about five inches too short. Once some tubby guy gets through cranking on the seat or pushing through the chair bottom, the keyboard of my computer hits me chest-high, making it impossible to use the desk for long.

Buns is up for another round of tweezing her brows at the magnifying mirror we affectionately refer to as her searchlight. But could she open the closet door to retrieve her makeup kit? Sure, but not until the bathroom door was closed. You would think that this hotel company, after making the same mistake over a few thousand rooms at another location, would figure it out. But the door arrangement in this hotel is exactly the same in their latest edition.

What's my point? If you ask the wrong questions, you are no better off than asking none at all.

My appendix fell out late one Friday afternoon. By Monday, stoicism no longer sufficed. Buns hauled me to the doctor who enrolled me in a special Appendectomy 101 course. I passed the time marveling at the number of fast-food deliveries that made it past the nurses, wondering how I could get in on the action. No one, except for the few too weak to defend themselves, even attempted to eat the godawful mess that passed as food.

By midweek, I was ready to climb the hospital walls, when there was a polite tapping on the door frame to my room.

"Come in!"

"Mr. Gross?"

"Yes."

"I'm from the food service department, and I would like to ask you a few questions, if you don't mind."

"Shoot." At least I had company.

"Are you getting served three times a day?"

"As regular as a clock."

"Is the hot food hot and the cold food cold?"

"No problem."

"Are you able to chew your food?"

"It was my appendix that they overhauled. My chewer is working just fine."

The sprite with the tiny voice and even smaller smile, carefully closed her notebook, stood quickly, smoothed her skirt, and said, "Thank you, Mr. Gross. We appreciate your input."

"Wait a minute!"

"Yes, sir?" The voice was a combination of puzzlement and concern.

"Don't you want to know how this stuff tastes?"

She opened her notebook, studied it in a glance, and looking pleased with herself, attempted to stand tall on the side of efficiency and all things corporate, saying, "No, sir! That's not one of our questions."

"Well, sit down and take a note!"

She grabbed a pen, opened her notebook, and started to write even before I launched—probably something to the effect of "Do not include psychiatric patients in future surveys!"

"Miss, if the food tastes like used shortening, it doesn't matter if it is delivered on time or that the hot food is hot and the cold food is cold. It doesn't matter if you can chew it, if after the first day you have figured out that it's not fit for man or beast. And, of course, the portions will be large enough. In fact, any of this mess is plenty if not too much! If I were colorblind, I would have no way telling this stuff apart. To me it's either red stuff or green stuff, neither of which I will put in my body.

"Write that down, please."

And I never saw her again. If you don't ask the right question, you cannot get the right answer!

You Have to Ask the Right Question . . .

. . . if you want to be certain you get the right answer.

It's almost a famous story, repeated so many times that I am beginning to think it as urban legend. The story is about the marketing director of a large hotel in downtown Chicago who marched into her boss's office and announced that according to her surveys nearly 100 percent of hotel guests would appreciate having a small television in the bathroom.

What she had failed to do was to ask the right question: "Would you be willing to pay an additional fee to have a television in your bathroom?" On resurveying the same crowd that reported they would appreciate a bathroom TV, almost none would actually be willing to pay for the privilege. But what they would pay for would be a full-size ironing board with a home-style steam iron!

The Peabody Hotel in Orlando is one hotel I know of that has bathroom television. For some oddball reason—maybe it was lack of space, maybe the bathroom television was an afterthought the small television is mounted right behind the commode. (Duh!)

While you were reading, Buns and I skipped out for a breath of fresh air. After all, even old people should have things to do on a Saturday night. So we walked and dipped two straws into a so-so vanilla shake before calling an end to our hot date. I'm back in the chair. She is ironing, pretty much in the dark. You see, the hotel is apparently on an energy kick, and though the sentiment is at the very least admirable, they may have taken it too far.

The light in the entryway to our room, the only place near to a plug and big enough for the task, must be all of 25 watts. That's fine to keep you from falling over luggage but impossible for creasing a shirtsleeve. I would have sat in the single, comfortable chair in the room (there must be a rule about two guests sitting at once), but someone, probably the energy czar, had removed the reading lamp. So, with two in a room, you can flip for the chair, and the winner is left in the dark.

This is not an inexpensive hotel. And I can prove it. The little light on the room telephone is flashing. I know what will happen if I give in to its call. "You are using XX Mail (like I care what brand of torture they are using)." What follows is a tutorial on how to customize your mailbox. Okay, let's see a show of hands, please, for all of you folks who personalize your hotel room voice message. I see . . . oh, there are two of you!

Everyone who doesn't want to chance missing an important message will stand, luggage in hand, bent over the telephone and cringing through another tutorial. Why? Because you know that at the very end of the recording, there may be messages, or at least one message, and chances are it's from someone claiming to be a member of the management team reading in monotone from a script suggesting that you call if there is anything they can do to make your stay a pleasant one.

As a matter of fact, there is! Put a button on my phone that lets me go straight to my messages without the tutorial. And while you are at it, stop calling my room with insincere drivel!

At the end of the message, we learn that we can "press 7 to clean up your messages." So I pressed 7.

"If you wish to delete your messages, press 1." And I pressed 1.

"If you are certain you wish to delete all of your messages, press 1 to confirm."

I pressed 1, already, you idiots!

One last shot and I'll leave the hotel boys alone. I have a dollar that says if I walk over to the bed and pull the covers back the top and bottom sheets will be tucked in together. It's an efficiency trick that makes dressing the bed faster since you handle both sheets at once. Yep, I was right. I pulled back the cover and undressed the bed all in one quick swoop.

Now here's the key point. Most of these tiny assaults on customers go unnoticed by the customers, at least consciously. I have the sneaking suspicion that these tiny insults—we call them microinsults—although they never actually show on the radar, are nevertheless noticed by customers, on some level.

We stayed at the Ritz Carlton in Orlando a few weeks ago. The Ritz pretty much sets the standard when it comes to customer service. But even the Ritz has its "duh" moments. When we walked into our room, we actually said, "Wow!" The room was perfect, the view was delightful, every "i" dotted and every "t" crossed. The bed was a monument to comfort, piled high with a rich down-filled duvet.

Wait a minute! Did I say Ritz Carlton in Orlando? As in Florida? With a heavy duvet?

In Florida you don't need bed covers from the Alps. You need air-conditioning. The only way we could be comfortable under that luscious pile of indulgence was to crank the AC to the bottom of the scale. And we couldn't bring ourselves to waste the energy required to ice up the room just so we could snuggle under the covers.

Unless you get your customers to talk, you may, with the best of intentions, be creating a microinsult. And I'll bet that the Ritz has yet to have a complaint about those wonderful beds. Still, unconsciously, someone may have felt just a twinge of guilt using the AC to turn their room into a meat locker!

You probably have never paid much attention to the snap-on caps on the shampoo bottles that make them near impossible to take home. You are probably used to removing a promotional card for breakfast from your pillow. You've learned to tolerate the room desk being unusable until the room service menu and the note from the housekeeper hinting for a tip are cleared.

But you will notice now. And when you peel back the covers, you're going to make a conscious decision about which company is really putting you first.

Microinsults rarely result in a complaint or even get a mention in casual conversation. But the customer is watching, recording, and deciding who is and who is not really on their side. So think about it. How do your customers perceive you, unconsciously?

I'll Say It Again . . .

If you ask the wrong question, you get the wrong answer! Too many customer-response systems force the customer to answer questions that aren't burning issues with the customer. If you would like to find out what your customers think about the new store layout, it is perfectly fine to ask—and you should! But consider that the new store layout may not be an issue with the customer. Read on to see what one surveyed customer revealed:

> . . . dirty bathrooms and no toilet paper in the stalls, toilet seats that are broken, and doors that have locks that are not working. One bathroom in particular has only one stall for the whole store and the latch is nonexistent. You need to bring tissue from home if you are planning to shop there. (Unfortunately, this store is close to my home, and I can walk there for my prescriptions.)

To use the bathroom you need to improvise and use the large green trash can to put in front of the door and hope that a lady who doesn't already know the situation doesn't barge in and catch you in a compromising position. So usually I have to yell, "There's someone in here!!" A voice from behind the door will respond, "OK," then I usually tell them about the garbage can doorstop.

Of course, after that I feel like my hands need to be autoclaved for germs because they don't have soap and the hand dryer blows only cold air.

Asking a lady who has just escaped a filthy toilet stall about her feelings for a new store layout isn't going to produce the most valuable insight. Ask the questions that are of interest to you, but always invite the customer to comment on issues that are important to him or her.

On the other hand, it's too easy to ask the obvious question. Unfortunately, the obvious question is not always likely to produce the information you really need. For example, say you want to create a local marketing campaign and use direct mail. The easiest thing to do is look at your customer database, determine the area from which you draw the bulk of your customers, and target that area for a mail drop. But unless you also compare addresses with purchases, you may miss the fact that your highest-profit customers actually live in a different part of town. It may be more profitable to focus your marketing dollars differently. But you won't know unless you ask the right question.

Pay Attention to Language

It's easy to assume you have asked the right question, when in fact you are way off the mark. What happens if you ask, "Which store do you think is best for customer service?" That question yields an entirely different data set than, "Of the stores you shop most often, which gives the best customer service?" And that question is entirely different from, "Have you ever changed stores because of poor customer service?" or even, "Have you ever switched to a new store because of its reputation for great customer service?"

MAKE THE CORRECT INTERPRETATION

My good friend Fred Vang, the automotive consultant who lives on a mountaintop in Santa Fe, New Mexico, makes a living off of car dealers who have burned so many customers that smart folks do anything they can to avoid being attacked in a showroom. When they go to Fred, he listens to their needs, recommends the perfect vehicle, and then sets out to arrange the best deal possible.

You could say that Fred makes a very good living by listening to his customers. In his salad days as a car salesman for a BMW dealership, Fred was approached by a woman who said right up front that she was looking for a safe vehicle. Fred went right to work and arranged for her to see a video describing the safety features of the latest models. She saw graphics highlighting the construction details, and she watched footage of the crash test dummies hard at work. In the end, she went elsewhere and purchased an underpowered, very conservative economy car! Do you have any idea what the basis for her decision was?

It turned out that the woman was not looking for a vehicle that could survive a crash. What she really wanted was a vehicle that would not get *into* a crash in the first place. She didn't want survivability; she wanted avoidance. And in her mind, slow speed and little power equated to safety.

Then there was the pickle car. Fred had a client who had an unquenchable craving for pickles—not the eating kind, the driving kind. As I recall the story, Nissan released a series of cars painted a color that can only be described as pickle green. (I've actually seen this car, and pickle green is really too kind a description. It's flat out u-g-l-y!)

Beauty is in the eye of the beholder, and Fred's client wanted pickle green. Unfortunately for the client, not for the rest of us, Nissan had wisely discontinued the practice of pickling its cars. But Fred was listening, and he found one last pickle to purchase. Another satisfied customer!

- Car dealership salespersons who are like vultures. Even though you tell them you are just looking or cannot afford to purchase right now, they have the tendency to talk you into it anyway! They promise you will be able to afford the car even if you have no income! It's insane!
- Car salespersons who don't know about the product they are selling. When we purchased a new Chevy 4X4, the first salesman (it was a man) didn't even know the size of the engine! My husband

had to explain how to count cylinders on the engine to determine if it is a six or an eight. The next guy knew a little more but couldn't answer a question about vehicle controls. Finally, they sent out a guy (yes, I do mean another man) that said he had been working at the dealership for four years. When we asked if the rear seats came out or laid flat, it took him 15 minutes of trying and another 5 minutes to call for help. Needless to say, we didn't purchase from this dealership.

+ Intelligent salespeople
− Loud car commercials, especially screaming about used cars
− Stupid ads. This is a big turnoff. Most TV commercials are not realistic and tend toward the idiotic side by downplaying a person's intelligence. It would be nice if the public had a place to express their feelings about commercials.
+ I like 0 percent financing offers.
+ Salespersons who pay attention. My best experience was when I was shopping for a car. I thought all I could spend was $8,000 and was looking for a used car close to that amount. When I walked into an Acura dealership, the salesman greeted me and asked my name and what I needed. He showed me a car in my price range that I did not like. I noticed an Integra on the lot, asked about it, and was offered a test-drive. I said no, I just wanted to sit in it. He answered my questions and I left the dealership. For three months, I looked at other dealers but kept thinking about the Integra. I returned to the Acura dealership. When I walked through the door, the same salesman was working. He looked up, smiled, called me by name, and said, "I see you've come to pick up your Integra." And I did!

TAKE ACTION

Years ago, we were franchisees of a major fast-food restaurant chain. It was required by contract that we make customer comment cards available to our guests. The cards were postage prepaid, and it was our habit to include them with most orders. They went out by the hundreds, but not a single one ever made it back to us. That was puzzling, to say the least.

Walking through the corporate offices one sunny day, I noticed a huge pile of familiar yellow cards. They were comment cards. Hundreds of them, maybe thousands! I attacked the pile and, sure enough, there was one from our restaurant, then another, and soon a handful, and I was just skimming the surface of the pile!

"What's with this?" I shouted.

"Tell Us cards." This from the department secretary who spoke as if I had lost my mind.

"There must be thousands of them!"

"I know," whined the woman with more responsibility than time.

"Why haven't you been sending them to me?" I knew the answer but just wanted to hear it directly.

"Too many cards, too little time. Too many more important things. Too bad."

Yes, it was too bad. The handful of comment cards that needed my personal attention to remedy errors or slights had by now aged beyond recovery. A minor complaint that had been left to age in the dark corner of the secretary's office was by now a major slight, further evidence that we didn't care about the customer then and didn't care about the customer now.

Feedback delayed loses its value.

Evidence of Listening

Worse than not asking is asking without listening. Always respond to customer's input either individually or as a group. Promise to post the survey results on the Web or to follow up with a mass e-mail. No matter how you respond, make it clear that you have received and considered their input.

Make It Personal

One of the biggest mistakes you can make in customer relationship management is to treat input that was sincerely offered as inconsequential. That's what makes form letters so dangerous. They are easy to use but deadly when it comes to relationships. Form letters say, "Yeah, yeah, we've heard this all before. Now be a nice customer and go away." Form letters are a form of disrespect, just what you need for a customer who may already be thinking about jumping ship.

Try complaining to Dell. The order for this very computer was so thoroughly botched that we had to cancel and start over. I'm still not certain that the computer I received is actually the computer I ordered. Did I complain? I tried. Did they listen? Not even. I e-mailed a complaint.

They e-mailed a form for me to complete that had nothing to do with what I had experienced. I concluded that Dell didn't care. Now, as a businessperson, I know that is not true. Dell does care. But some genius in a windowless cubicle had the bright idea to use technology for everything, including listening to customers. It can work, but you have to be careful and the operative word is this—*personal.*

Take It from the Top

Customers aren't responsible for managing your business; it's your job to present the offer (product, price, place, and people). The only job of the market is to accept or not accept the offer. Customers are not obligated to sing your praises when your offer is on target, nor are they restricted from telling the world when they think your offer stinks.

When customers talk, they are doing us a favor. Usually talking customers expect only one thing in return—action.

Customers talk largely because they want to remain our customers. They talk because changing their buying habits has its own set of inconveniences and uncertainties. Often, what our customers are saying is, "I really want to remain your customer, and I will, if you will just fix . . . "

Customers want to know that they have been heard. They hate feeling as though they are hollering down a well. They want their message to go all the way to the top.

Customer feedback should always be acknowledged by the highest officer in the company. Why? Because it communicates to the customer that the complaint was heard by someone who can DO something! Remember, the purpose of most legitimate complaints is to help you help them remain a customer.

Feedback Cards

We found Max & Erma's on a visit to Cincinnati and were blown away. Judging by the size of the Monday night crowd, we weren't the only ones impressed. As part of his greeting, our server asked, "Is this your first time at Max & Erma's?" We said yes, he thanked us for giving them a try, and we gave the exchange no further thought, other than to comment that Max & Erma had done a great job training.

After a killer meal, our check was delivered by a pleasant young woman who identified herself as an assistant manager, who verified that we were first-timers and surprised us with a guest comment card that included a $5 voucher for our next visit. What kind of response do you think they get on an offer like this?

As an aside, how much do you figure is the actual cost of the offer? If the guest check average is a conservative $12.50 and the average party is two guests, then we are talking about a 20 percent discount on a $25.00 check. Food cost is in the neighborhood of 35 percent, which leaves $11.25 to cover labor and overhead—plenty! Now figure that since there is a significant discount involved, the guests are likely to return much sooner than expected, which is itself an act of building a Max & Erma's habit.

But what if the guest experience had been a poor one? This same couple, expected to be monthly guests representing $300 in annual sales, could be salvaged simply because someone had the foresight to ask and was willing to risk $1.75. Talking to customers pays!

Comment cards are a little old-fashioned but still around because they are inexpensive and they work—but only if you do them right.

Effective guest comments require that . . .

- You ask the right guest.
- You ask the right questions and ask them right.
- There is evidence that you are listening.
- There is immediate response.
- The response comes from a high level.
- The response is individualized and personal.

Data without action is wasted information. If you are going to collect it, have the courage to act on it. Too often companies collect data, are frightened by it, and then decide to ignore it. Sometimes, they blame the data collection process, but more often they blame the consumers who are labeled as not understanding the concept.

The customer is never wrong, even though he or she may not be right. If the customer thinks it, it is so.

A small case in point is okra. This is just an opinion, but I think okra is proof that God has a sense of humor. "Well, the oysters turned out pretty good. Tomorrow I'll make the vegetable equivalent." (I'm not certain of the scriptural reference.) The point is, I wouldn't eat that stuff on a bet. But when we ran a fast-food fried chicken franchise, we sold that slimy vegetable by the boatload.

The customer is never wrong, even though he or she is not right.

If the customer says the store is too cold, it's too cold. If the customer says, "I want to buy baggy pants so large it looks like I mugged my father," you'd better get them in stock. If the customer wants fried okra, give it to him! You can talk bad about customers when you write your first book! Whatever the customer wants, give it to him. Whatever the customer's problem is, solve it for her. When the customer talks, listen respectfully.

The customer is never wrong, even though he or she may not be right.

But you won't find out what the customer is thinking unless you ask, listen, act, and ask again.

Have a Coke and a . . .

Here's another quick example, Coca-Cola Red Lounges. The forward thinkers at Coke noticed (that's another way of listening) that fans of American Idol were intrigued when winners of a Coke-sponsored contest got to watch the final episode while sitting on the set's "Red Couch." It was an easy leap to imagine Coca-Cola customers of all stripes would enjoy the camaraderie of sharing an ice-cold Coke while lounging around with their friends.

Voila! Coca-Cola Red Lounges recently debuted in malls in Illinois and Los Angeles. Coke decided to hang with their young customers, who are notorious for hanging at the local mall. Equipped with custom-built furniture, plenty of exclusive audio and video programming, games, and more from FUSE, G4, Sony, and ESPN, the lounges serve as teen-targeted events and, not surprisingly, listening posts for a new generation of Coca-Cola customers.

Kohl's has had their ear to the ground and discovered an untapped potential in a clothing line for tweens, that awkward age when young girls are about to leap directly from age 9 to age 29 with no steps in between, when every 10-year-old wants to change her name to Brittany.

Kohl's discovered that these girls want clothes their way, and we're not talking only fashion. They want an experience that includes music and an integrated Web site, in addition to the customized line of apparel and accessories that has been branded everGirl. To seal the deal with the highly targeted market, an everGirl song and music video were released by the all-girl band, PLAY.

And who do you suppose is Kohl's partner? Nickelodeon, of course!

Mastering the Art of the Personal Intercept

I guess it was Tom Peters who coined the term, "a blinding flash of obvious." Speaker Scott McCain tells a hilarious story about rushing around town in a late-night emergency search for cufflinks, only to be zinged by a clerk who suggested that rather than attempt to create cufflinks where there were none, it might be easier to just buy a new shirt.

That's the way business is. Sometimes the answer to our biggest problems is right in front of us. All we need to do is look or, as may be the case, listen.

At Sporty's, we practice what we call the three impossibles. It should be impossible to visit without being greeted by an owner or a manager. It should be impossible to leave without feeling satisfied with your experience. And it should be impossible to leave without being thanked for your business.

It's simple, maybe even quaint, but oh, is it powerful. We're all over our customers like white on rice. They tell us how we are doing in no uncertain terms for two reasons: first, because they know us, and second, because we ask.

Intercept a guest and ask a dumb-head question like, "Is everything all right?" and you will get the totally useless response of "Fine, thank you." What a waste of time. But ask a question that requires a little introspection, and you'll get a gold mine of actionable data:

- "How did you decide to come to Sporty's tonight?"
- "What other restaurants do you frequent?"
- "Why do you like them?"
- "What could we do to make this an even better place?"

These questions will get you results.

Once your service concept is defined and translated into policy and procedure, management is left with two simple-yet-difficult-to-execute responsibilities—build strong customer relationships (including internal customers) and lead by example.

Customers will talk to you anytime. But they won't tell you something of value unless they think they know you. The value of data is based on trust. You can't build trustworthy relationships while sitting in the office. Smart managers spend as much time as possible belly-to-belly with their customers. When they do, they increase the chances of getting honest, candid, useful feedback from the folks who pay the bills. At the same time, they demonstrate to the staff how customers expect to be treated.

Air Time

I had given up on Continental Airlines years ago after a series of poor service experiences. It wasn't the lost baggage or the misconnections or the rude service. I can handle that. I couldn't tolerate being ignored when I politely complained, so I fired them in a quiet ceremony when I called our corporate travel agent and said, "No more."

A few years went by, and I began to notice that passengers getting off Continental flights no longer seemed agitated, and flight attendants leaving their flights no longer seemed mentally beat. Then I read that Continental had earned a service award, an on-time award, and a baggage handling award. Maybe they are worth another try. Nah, not yet.

A name began to connect with this once "Proud Bird with a Golden Tail": Gordon Bethune, a new guy and a different sort of leader. I heard he listened, not just to customers but to employees as well. I read that the turning point actually had a date and time attached to it. Bethune threw a party—at his home—for 100 of the airline's elite-level One Pass members. (They probably lived in Houston and Continental was their airline by default, but nonetheless it was above and beyond.) At the party, Bethune essentially apologized for the airline's decline and promised to do something about it.

News of the party and the apology swept through the ranks of Continental employees. It sent a message that said Continental was going to do what customers wanted them to do: "Work hard. Fly right."

Build Trust Leading by Example

Tom Coughlin, president of stores for Wal-Mart, is a leader who demonstrates this philosophy. Some years ago, I was scheduled to speak to several thousand Wal-Mart managers and, in the course of doing my due diligence, I called for Tom the day before Thanksgiving. And to be blunt, I didn't expect Tom to be in. (What I really wanted to do was to move responsibility for carrying the phone tag ball from my desk to his.)

"Mr. Coughlin is not in this afternoon," said the soft southern accent at the other end of the line.

"I guess he got a head start on turkey and football."

"Oh, no!" said the voice, obviously shocked that I would think the boss was human. "No, sir! He's out amongst them!" In regular English, she meant that Tom was out working the stores on what is one of the busiest days in retailing. Think about it. Wal-Mart has maybe three million employees, and this guy, this one middle-aged guy, thinks he makes a difference by bagging a few groceries at some Podunk Wal-Mart Supercenter?

You bet your stock option he does!

Herb Kelleher was famous among the Southwest Airlines employees, his internal customers, for working as a baggage handler on that same day before Thanksgiving, appropriately called Black Wednesday in the airline business.

What were these guys thinking? My guess is that these two wily leaders knew very well that being out among their employees was a surefire way to build trust, while discovering firsthand about life in the real world.

So, the first step for you to take is to get "out amongst them."

Step number two is to ask the right questions. We talk elsewhere about what are the right questions, but for now let's mention what has to be the world's stupidest question: "Did you find everything all right?"

Let's see. Option one. I am plowing along behind a shopping cart piled high with purchases. And you want to know if I found everything? Option two is I am leaving your store with absolutely nothing in my hand. Isn't it pretty darned obvious that I either did not find what I wanted or found it but just wasn't ready to buy it?

Do this. Get in front of your customers at every opportunity and, once you are there, ask them questions that yield real, actionable data rather than hackneyed replies intended to dismiss. Talk to customers who have made purchases to find out why they bought. You may be surprised to discover that the killer feature you thought would drive sales to new records had little or no impact on the buying decision.

Customers purchase for their own reasons, not yours.

Talk to customers who leave without making a purchase. Ask them where, when, what, and how they are likely to decide to open their wallets. You may find you need a new game plan.

"I noticed that you didn't get a dessert tonight."

"These portions are so big, we haven't got room for more."

"Did you see the Brownie Bite? We created it just for folks like you. It's a little bitty brownie that we have baked locally by the Clark Family Bakery, topped by a melon scoop of Blue Bell vanilla ice cream, and finished with a rosette of whipped cream and a drizzle of Hershey's chocolate! Sound good?"

And, here was the take-home for the boss—big portions may be affecting dessert sales. Maybe we should tell the customers about the desserts up front and suggest they save room or be thinking about choosing a dessert to share!

Earning the Right to Speak Is . . .

Easy. Earning the right to be heard is priceless!

Earning trust is becoming more difficult, thanks to technology that allows us to hear our customers even when they are not speaking directly to us.

Senator Patrick Leahy has asked for congressional hearings on privacy issues surrounding the new RFID (radio frequency identification) technology. RFID involves placing a small microchip on a product or its packaging that amounts to a tiny radio transmitter. The RFID makes it possible to track the location of inventory in real time.

Of particular concern were tests of RFID technology by Gillette and Procter & Gamble. In these tests, RFID chips allowed scanners located many miles from the monitoring site to track razor and lipstick inventories. It's no longer theory; a manufacturer or other agency can track your use of RFID products without your knowledge.

The senator said, "The need to draw some lines is already becoming clear." He called RFID tracking devices "surveillance technology."

Wal-Mart, the undisputed king of distribution technology, is requiring most of its top 100 suppliers to be RFID-capable by early 2005, and all of its suppliers will be required to tag pallets and cases by the end of 2006.

RFID is by no means all "downside" for the consumer; it's just a matter of trade-off. In exchange for a small loss of privacy, consumers can expect lower prices, better products (thanks to research enhanced by RFID data collection), and perhaps a few perks, such as shorter lines and special offers for frequent shoppers. Once the privacy issues are resolved, the only missing technology is imagination.

The senator acknowledged that the technology "may be a good idea for a retailer to use to manage inventory," but said that the tags should not be put on goods for sale without the consumer's knowledge, without knowing how to deactivate them, and without knowing what information would be collected and how it would be used and safeguarded. Meanwhile, testing by many consumer packaged-goods companies and retailers is well underway. These companies hope to save millions of dollars by automating the retail supply chain and preventing theft via RFID tags. Tests include imbedding the chips in pallets and cases to track the flow and inventory of goods. An initial plan to track individual packages was squashed after privacy advocates cried foul.

Wal-Mart has been forced to make certain accommodations as it works to roll out the program. For example, Wal-Mart revised its schedule for drugmakers from a March deadline to the end of June, the *New York Times* reported. Wal-Mart has already signed up at least 138 manufacturers to participate in RFID tagging. Other retailers, including Metro AG and Albertsons, are following suit.

"There is no downside to a public dialogue about these issues, but there are many dangers in waiting too long to start," Leahy said. "We need clear communication about the goals, plans, and uses of the technology, so that we can think in advance about the best ways to encourage innovation, while conserving the public's right to privacy."

Is it a surprise that the most successful retailers are those who know how to listen when customers talk?

For more information, visit http://www.whencustomerstalk.com.

6

HOW CUSTOMERS WANT TO BE SERVED

"I would like to witness price drops in person just as they appear on TV when the Wal-Mart yellow smiley face does its thing."

+ I like salespeople who let you browse when you say you are just looking.
− You no more get in the door, and a salesperson wants to know if he or she can help you with something!
− I just like to be left alone to look around; if I need help I will ask for it.
+ Help but only when I need it
− Salespersons who follow you around
− Clerks who insist on helping even after I have declined their offer
− Any store where sales staff is so pushy you almost have to be mean to them or leave the store to get any relief!
− Associates who look at you and hurry off, so they won't have to help you
− Associates who never say anything, no thank you, how are you doing, or anything
+ Clerks who are willing to call another store to find what you want and then offer to have it shipped to you

+ Clerks who are willing to find out an answer, even if they don't know it off the top of their head
- It's bad when I know more about a sales promotion than the sales-people do!
- Pushy customers
+ Stores that go out of their way to get the exact product you want

•   •   •   •   •

"Once when I was looking for a nice suit to wear to a friend's wedding, I wandered into a high-class men's apparel store. As I looked at several expensive suits, a salesman asked what I was doing. I told him about the wedding and that I wanted to wear a knockout suit.

"He looked me up and down and told me that he didn't think the store had what I was looking for. I knew why. I was wearing jeans with holes and a T-shirt. While pulling out my wallet, I informed the salesman that he should not judge people by what they are wearing and waved a wad of Bens (hundred-dollar bills) under his nose.

"A supervisor appeared and apologized, but I took my money down the mall and spent it elsewhere."

•   •   •   •   •

"As the owner of a relatively large warehouse that distributes automotive products over 17 states, I live a rather comfortable life, which includes a summer home located on a tree farm in southern Indiana. My mother, who is very well off, was visiting and asked me to assist her in buying a new car. She had been driving a Cadillac but felt she wanted something slightly smaller this time.

"I felt I needed to assist her but was not really dressed for the chore, because I had been moving fences for the horse all day. I nevertheless agreed and proceeded to the local dealer. We were greeted after a time and, as we walked through the showroom, I noticed an older Mercedes convertible. I had been wanting a new toy since I had sold my Corvette a year or so before. I asked the salesman how much the Mercedes might be.

"He must have prejudged my ability to pay, because he replied, "If you have to ask, you probably couldn't afford it." Since the dealer was a friend of mine, I let the comment drop, left the store, and made an all-cash purchase with the competition."

•   •   •   •   •

- − Employees who act as if you are an inconvenience when you ask for directions
- + Those who treat you as a special person
- − Salespeople too busy with personal conversations to help you
- − Salespeople who try to sell you more than you want or need
- + Well-trained salespeople who are easy to find on the sales floor
- − Salespersons who work on commission
- + Being willing to tell you that their product may not be the best choice
- − Sales associates who refuse to make eye contact
- − People who cannot count change and who are lost if a register goes down
- + Any salesperson who makes eye contact and can count change
- + Friendly people who smile, care about customers, and enjoy their work
- − Employees who talk to other employees about personal issues while they are ringing me up
- + Recognizing that I am a regular customer

• • • • •

"I believe the customer who has left the house and gone to the trouble of coming to your store deserves service before customers who call on the phone. Salespeople should ignore ringing phones or put them on hold until the customer at the register is taken care of."

• • • • •

"As a veteran of almost 50 years in the retail and government food industry, I never cease to be amazed at the lack of attention or downright discourtesy given to customers who are in the store to spend money and who therefore pay the salaries of the employees.

"Too many employees act as if they are doing you a favor by shopping at that store. I attribute this performance directly to lack of proper management. Many years ago, I was told by a senior manager that he could enter a store and, after standing just inside the selling area for five or ten minutes, would know the personality of the top management of that location. I have found this to be so true.

"If employees are smiling at customers, offering to pick up that piece of paper that just fell on the floor, and so on, you can be assured you are witnessing the result of attentive, fair-minded management that encourages the staff to provide customers with the most pleasant service experience possible."

• • • • •

"There is a checker at our grocery store whose face would most likely crack if she smiled. I actually avoid her checkout line. Of course, that is probably what she wants me to do."

• • • • •

- − When someone who works for a store I'm shopping curses
- − Young girls with nose rings. I want to hand them a Kleenex.
- − Checkout clerks who chew gum with their mouths open
- − Clerks with straggly hair and unkempt clothing that chew gum
- − Not treating employees well in front of customers
- − Clerks on the phone with their friends
- − Being cashed out by someone having a complex conversation with either another cashier or, worse, on the cell phone
- − Salespeople who don't speak English are a big turnoff.
- − Clerks who walk right by you when they know you need help
- − Being called honey or sweetie
- − Having our group addressed as guys
- − Being ignored in a hardware store because you are a woman
- − Handing over money I have worked hard for to someone who is disrespectful
- + Cashiers who say hello and thank you
- − Retailers who ask for your address and phone number or zip code
- − Clerks who do not say one word during an entire transaction. I had to look at the register screen to find out how much to pay.
- − When restaurant servers ask if you want change
- + When a cashier or clerk gives me a friendly smile
- − Pushing extended warranties
- − Out-of-stock sale items, especially right after the sale is announced. They said they only had to have one in stock to run the ad. It's a great way to get customers in the store once but once will be enough!

• • • • •

"I hate bad service, especially when it's from a store I want to shop regularly. My son and I went to check it out opening day of a new T.J. Maxx store. At the time, he was a young man and looked like a teenager. He had on a large bulky coat with many pockets and was also carrying a bag from the store we had just shopped.

"At one side of the store were all of the suits and higher-ups from the company admiring their new store. The security lady told my son he had to take the bag to the front of the store and leave it at the counter. This had never happened to him or me at any other store. My take on the situation was that the security person was being overzealous in order to show the brass she was on the ball for shoplifters.

"We turned around and walked out, and T.J. Maxx has never gotten another penny from me."

•   •   •   •   •

+ The people at Safeway are very nice and that's why I started shopping there.

+ Whole Foods Market and Safeway stores have very friendly, helpful checkers of all ages and ethnicities. Both stores have good service and short lines.

+ Let me look, offer to help, and then leave me alone unless I ask for help again. Dillard's is very good at this.

+ Home Depot has salesclerks who actually know the locations of merchandise, answer questions in a friendly manner, and truly make shopping a pleasure.

+ I like to ask questions in a home improvement store and get answers I actually understand. Lowe's is good at this.

+ Salesclerks at Foleys always thank you by name when you purchase by credit card.

+ I like to receive specialized assistance and training in a home remodeling project. The best retailer in this regard is Home Depot.

| Smaller mom-and-pop stores are best, as they are happy to see you shop with them.

− I can't stand high-end places like Neiman Marcus and Lord & Taylor that sell junk at ridiculous prices trying to be trendy.

− Furniture and car salespeople are the worst!

+ When I am looking at electronics, I like for salespeople to ask if I have questions and, if they don't know the answers, find someone who does. (Wal-Mart)

+ I like stores that offer senior discounts. Kohl's is great about this. I just qualified! We deserve a break!

− Best Buy is awful. The salespeople are pushy and, worse, are dumb. They know nothing about the product they're selling, and they constantly push service contracts that you don't need or want.

- − On discovering an item is out of stock, the salesperson tries to push me into buying something else instead of what I wanted. I've had this experience at Best Buy.
- + Barnes & Noble has a dedicated information center with a number of helpful salespeople.
- + Babies R Us associates are smart, funny, and helpful.
- − Some furniture stores spend years going out of business.
- + Sears has frequent sales and stands behind its products.
- − Shoe salespeople who don't have the size you request but bring out shoes in sizes that aren't even close!

• • • • •

"I will drive 20 miles to grocery shop at AJ's Fine Foods. It has soft lighting and quality foods. I appreciate premade salads and dinners, as I don't have time to make them myself. (I'm spending too much time on-line completing surveys!)

"The most-offensive service I ever experienced was at 24 hour Fitness. The salesperson, assistant sales manager, and sales manager practically cornered me and gave me a panic attack. I cried all the way home"

MAY I SAY WHO IS CALLING?

In 1953, Miss Alberta Allen looked at a sea of dirty faces in a hot, muggy schoolroom. I was one of those dirty-faced Kentuckians, sweating out the final few days of third grade, praying for a breeze or Superman to fly through the open window to save us.

I would bet Miss Allen couldn't in her wildest dreams imagine that anybody was paying attention or that anybody would remember. I was, and I do. Miss Allen said that a generation is about 25 years, and that meant there would be four generations to a century. She named them, speaking slowly and clearly in her best teacher diction and grammar. I'm assuming she was correct, then.

Sociologists say a generation is defined not by time but by a set of experiences and values shared by an age group. There was the depression generation, the great generation, followed by the baby boomers, and then, in spite of valiant attempts to name them, the idea of generations began to fall apart. This is because we got caught up in Miss Allen's 25-year theory—a theory that no longer works. Sociologists say that if we are to define a generation by a set of common values and experiences, we have to look more closely at our society. Values and experiences have been changing so rapidly that a new generation can now be declared every four years!

BIGresearch told me they had over 36 months of data to support their answer to one of my questions. In 1955, the boss would have said, "Come back when you know something, kid." But today I caught myself saying, "Thirty-six months? Don't you think that's a bit of overkill?" Time flies when you are changing.

Change has been a bit of a problem for marketers who say they are listening to customers, but do they really know who their customers are?

In 1989, something happened that should change our way of marketing for at least another two decades. For the first time in American history, in 1989 adults over 40 became the new customer majority. David Wolfe, author of *Ageless Marketing Strategies* (McGraw-Hill, 2003), says ". . . experts repeatedly remind us that aging boomers hate the idea of aging, so base your marketing to them on the values of youth." Bad advice!

Wolfe has a point. Most boomers I know, including myself and the one I live with, think aging gracefully is just fine. When Rums turned a still-beautiful 50, someone suggested I could trade her in for two 25-year-olds. The only thing worse than two 25-year-olds would be three of them!

If you are going to listen when customers talk, listen hardest to the older ones. As Willy Sutton would say: "That's where the money is!" Most of us boomers are quite comfortable with who we are and how we look. It's the marketers who have the problem!

In the coming decade, spending by the 45–65 group will increase by $329 billion, while the other age groups will decline in both size and spending power. That's the good news. The bad news, if you accept it, is that the group with the most bucks is also the group most resistant to traditional marketing. We know when an attempt is being made to manipulate us. We're less influenced by our peers and don't care what the Joneses have. It's not our first rodeo.

•   •   •   •   •

"Salespeople are typically more rude than in the past. I hate to stereotype, but 98 percent of the time, it is young people (16 to 24 years of age). I don't know if it is lack of training or bad upbringing. I'm only 33, but I feel that many young people just don't have respect for adults."

FISH WHERE THE FISHIN' IS . . .

If you want to talk to consumers, you've got to find them first. When we find customers, the first thing we ask out of habit is what media they use. (Houston, we have a problem. They're everywhere at the same time!) For example, 32.7 percent of males and 36.4 percent of females regularly watch television when they are online. If we change "regularly" to "occasionally," the numbers of both sexes involved in simultaneous media usage jump beyond 50 percent.

Are they paying attention? Simultaneous media users report that 51.1 percent give one medium more attention than the other, but a huge 32.9 percent claim to give both equal amounts of attention . . . or are they ignoring them equally?

Assuming today's consumers get any message at all, which ones are likely to motivate them to buy? Relevance seems to be the key, with 56.2 percent saying they preferred ads that "make me think about how the product would be useful to me."

The most influential medium (surprise) is word of mouth, according to 36.5 percent of the respondents. Coupons, say 23.1 percent, turn them on, and the third biggest motivator is television at 15.1 percent. Cable was fourth at 14.3 percent.

If word of mouth is the number-one medium influencing buying decisions, then you'll want to find and woo the 23 percent who regularly give advice to others on the purchase of goods and services. We call these folks influentials, and they are the most powerful media tool we have.

Who are the influentials in your business? Find them, woo them, and prosper.

ONLINE, OFF THE MARK

There is plenty of evidence that shoppers enjoy the convenience of shopping online. The price is usually right; there is often far more product information than in the stores; you can shop when you want; and there is never any need to fend off a pushy clerk by saying for the umpteenth time, "No, thanks, just looking."

That is using the Internet on customer terms, and that's the way it ought to be. According to pewinternet.org, companies that abuse customers by asking for sales online may be doing more harm than good. Fifty-two percent of e-mail users report that spam has made them somewhat suspicious of the medium. Seventy percent say spam makes using the Internet annoying. Seventy-five percent are bothered about being unable to stop spam.

And if you've ever wondered why so little written communication from customers includes e-mail addresses, it's because 73 percent don't feel comfortable giving out their e-mail address to businesses.

GETTING IT RIGHT

May I have the envelope, please?

We asked thousands of consumers what we consider to be the money question: "What types of services or offerings please you the most and make you want to shop most often at a particular retailer?" Translation: "What do you want from a shopping experience?"

The answer?

Knowledgeable/Helpful salespeople	41.4%
Courteous/Friendly/Caring staff	27.0%
Low prices and product information	18.3%
Merchandise organized and easy to find	8.8%
Fast checkout	4.5%
	100.0%

DOES IT MATTER?

You bet service matters! (When we say service, it is fair to substitute the word *experience*.) (See Figure 6.1.)

According to a survey by Amdocs (St. Louis), more than 80 percent of consumers would rather visit the dentist or sit in heavy traffic than deal with an unhelpful telephone representative. A survey by Gartner Inc. discovered that 53 percent of Internet users would switch or consider switching providers if unable to block spam. Georgetown University professor Ronald Goodstein says 40 percent of customers who change providers do so because of poor service. Our panel told us that given poor service, the likelihood of a repeat visit tapers off from the first mess-up.

FIGURE 6.1 *Regarding retail salespeople, have any of the following behaviors caused you to switch to another store?*

Rank	Top 10	Percent	
1	Rude behavior	13.3%	
2	Unfriendly manner	12.8%	
3	Ignore you	12.7%	
4	Are not around to help you	11.7%	
5	Watching you like a hawk/follow you around store	10.8%	
6	Not knowledgeable about product or store	10.5%	
7	Treat you as stupid or look down on you	8.9%	
8	Pushy personality	7.9%	
9	Constantly asking you if you need help	5.6%	
10	Sloppy looking	4.5%	
		98.7%	
Recap			
Bad manners	Rude/Unfriendly/Condescending	35.0%	Bad contact
Absent	Ignore you/Not around	24.5%	No contact
Space invader	Pushy/Like a hawk/Constantly asking to help	24.3%	Too much contact
		83.8%	

Source: BIGresearch, June 2004 (n = 8,701).

How many instances of poor service does it take for you to change service providers?

1	16.9%
2	40.6%
3	28.0%
4 or more	14.3%

WHAT SERVERS SAY

For fun we asked our panel what they thought was the root cause of poor service and got a few surprising answers. In order of importance, our panel of customers said that poor service is caused by:

1. Servers who don't care
2. Servers who aren't properly trained

3. Bosses who fail to schedule sufficient help
4. Customers who are rude
5. Customers who are impatient

Of the five reasons listed, the two most interesting are numbers 4 and 5. Customers actually blame themselves, at least in part. (If it's the second time for getting poor service, you can't say you weren't warned!) Why do you suppose customers would blame themselves for poor service? I think it's because most who live in the real world are servers when they aren't busy being served.

Our cooks at Sporty's also dine out. Our daytime dishwasher is currently in the hospital, where he is busy being a consumer of health care. And one of our servers, a true fashion plate, donates a good chunk of her tip money to the nice folks at the mall. We're almost all servers at one time, and we know from personal experience that servers exercise a great deal of latitude over how warm and fuzzy or shoulder-turning cold the service will be.

Can I throw in a view from the other side of the counter? I work in retail sales and the major turnoff for me is the customer who won't stop talking on the cell phone long enough to acknowledge that a real flesh-and-blood person is standing in front of them.

More than once a customer has come into the store, found multiple items to purchase, taken them to the register, checked out, and left the store without once interrupting their phone conversation.

CONSUMERS WANT RESPECT

PROMO Xtra (April 20, 2004) landed in my electronic in-basket with the latest survey from *Yankelovich Monitor* and a headline that said consumers want to be respected by marketers. Consumers want you to respect their dollars. They work hard for their money and rightfully want something of value in return. Customers want you to respect their time and the effort they made to visit your store. They want to be respected as individuals; they want their privacy protected; and they want you to respect their intelligence. Says the e-zine: "Consumer resistance to marketing is at an all-time high."

A study by Yankelovich Partners (Chapel Hill, NC) reports a backlash among consumers has made marketing efforts of all sorts less effective. Cited among the reasons are, "the saturated marketplace, intrusiveness of advertising and promotions, and lack of appropriate targeting." Over 60 percent of those surveyed are suspicious of the motives of advertisers, and it is these same folks who are at least interested in the idea of new regulations to limit marketing and advertising. Nearly 70 percent are interested in advertising-blocking technology, such as devices that skip commercials and eliminate pop-ups.

A whopping one-third of those surveyed said they would pay to live in an ad-free world. The days of wall-to-wall market saturation are fast coming to an end. The future will see a world where consumers are compensated in some way for their attention.

IN THE MOOD

Go ahead. Watch 'em. They saunter into the store, visually and tactilely graze the entire spread, and then suddenly bolt for the door as if their tails were on fire. You have just witnessed what happens when the customer shifts from the shopping mood to the leaving mood. Like a bad relationship that lasted way too long, customers, once satisfied, can't wait to leave.

Woe be unto those who make checkout an agony. They spend millions on creating the ultimate buying environment, and a few more millions in marketing to drag the customers through the door, and then spoil it all by hiring a semiliterate, gum-chewing cashier who might disappear if she actually made eye contact.

Customers told us that checkout is the critical choke point in all of retailing. It's quite possible that checkout is the first and last opportunity for human contact. What kind of an experience do you want to offer?

Interesting research by Richard Chase and Sriram Dasu (*Harvard Business Review,* June, 2001) suggests that the last point of customer contact may be the most important. One important discovery made by the researchers is the importance of sequence in determining the customer's overall feelings about the service experience. Customers prefer service that improves as the experience unfolds.

Inconvenient parking, long waits in line, encounters with displeasing policies all seem less negative when encountered early in the experience. Chase and Dasu say that last impressions, not initial ones, dominate the customer's feelings about the experience.

Daniel Kahneman, a Princeton University professor of psychology, specializes in cognitive psychology. In 1993, he conducted an experiment requiring subjects to choose between two unpleasant experiences.

In the first, participants were asked to put their hands into cold water (57 degrees F) for a full minute. The other exercise was identical except that the subjects followed the 57-degree immersion with an additional 30 seconds in 59-degree water—a full 50 percent increase in the time of discomfort mitigated only by a two-degree increase in temperature.

When asked which of the two experiences they would prefer to repeat, an amazing 70 percent of the participants said they would repeat the second one, even though the temperature difference was only slightly warmer by two degrees and even though the time of immersion was a full 50 percent longer!

Kahneman must be over 50, because his next experiment involved experiencing a colonoscopy. I guess he figured that as long as he was there, he may as well harvest the data. Kahneman's researchers decided to test the theory that the last impression really does have the greatest influence on feelings about the entire experience. They instructed medical technicians to leave the colonoscope in place for a full minute after the procedure was completed. This decreased the amount of discomfort at the end. Patients reported a significant improvement in their perceptions of the experience.

Stuff yourself into a regional jet for a couple of hours of cramped, noisy flying and predict how you are going to feel on arrival. Add in the likelihood that you will wait in quickly rising temperatures, while the ground crew unloads gate-checked baggage. How do you think this will influence your feelings about regional jets and the airlines that fly them?

Now, what if at the bottom of the aircraft steps you were greeted by a sharply uniformed, smiling airline employee who offered you a delicious fruit smoothie? Feels good just reading about it!

At Sporty's, on rainy days, we are certain to pop open a colorful golf umbrella to escort our guests to (and from!) their automobiles. When they get back to the office, what do you think they will be talking about?

Once the guest is in the leaving mood, make it fast, make it painless, and don't forget. It's showtime!

AT THE REGISTER

"How would you like to pay for this? Check, credit card, store credit card, debit card, store cash card . . . aluminum cans?"

In the 1950s, there were only two choices, cash or occasionally layaway. With layaway, you couldn't actually take the merchandise. Instead, it was placed along with other layaway merchandise on a shelf. Sometimes, when you stopped in on Friday to make your payment, you could see the object of your heart's desire, but you couldn't touch it. And you darned sure wouldn't take it until your balance and patience both reached zero.

Can you imagine telling a customer to wait until he or she can actually pay for something today? Try renting a car or even a hotel room with cash. Expect the third degree. It hasn't been too many years since we heard, "May I see your credit card and some other form of identification?" For most purchases, the credit card is the identification!

WHAT'S MY MOTIVE?

Getting consumers to buy on credit is easy. Getting them to buy credit from you is the hard part. Different incentives are necessary for different groups of consumers. Lower interest rates, cash-back programs, special discounts, and airline miles are some of the incentives that work. Piling on airline miles works especially well with the affluent customer, but overall this perk ranks at the bottom of the list.

The question is, Do these incentive programs really work? Yes, tactically, but probably no, strategically. Yes, consumers will sign up for a card that entitles them to free shipping, but they will also sign up for another card good for special bonuses or cash back. The incentive programs would be killers if there were a limit to the number of credit cards a customer could possess. But there is no limit, and consumers know it.

My Sears card has been in my top desk drawer for at least ten years. I'm saving it for a huge Craftsman tool orgy . . . someday. My Aircraft Pilots and Owners Association credit card is in my flight bag. It earns me a 5 percent rebate on fuel for my airplane up to $300 annually. When we reach the $300 level, I'll start with my American Airlines Visa card or my Southwest Airlines Visa card, so I can earn AA miles or free tickets on Southwest.

Sixty-two percent of our respondents said lower the interest and they would use their cards even more. (See Figure 6.2.) Many are responding to 0 percent introductory interest rate offers simply to transfer credit from higher-interest cards. When the introductory rates go up, the customer will go away. Credit card companies are going to have to find a way to make money on something other than high interest rates.

FIGURE 6.2 *Low Interest Rates Key to Increasing Card Use*

Low Interest Rates Key to Increasing Card Use

What would motivate you to use a credit card more?

Legend: ■ $50K+ Households   □ All

Category	$50K+ Households	All
Lower interest	61%	62%
Discounts	41%	39%
Cash-back	54%	51%
Airline miles	24%	17%
Free shipping	30%	28%
Reward/Point programs	46%	40%

Totals exceed 100 percent due to multiple answers.
Source: STORES 2003 Consumer Credit Survey, conducted by BIGresearch.

SOMEBODY HELP ME!

The opening scene is of a family barbeque in an obviously affluent neighborhood. The man of the family is telling about his new house, new automobile, membership in the country club, and other signs of living the good life. He ends the scene by saying, "Somebody help me, please. I'm up to my eyeballs in debt."

Watch CNN for ten minutes and no doubt you'll see that goofy banker lose another loan to Ditech. It's the world's most irritating commercial, but there it is, airing what seems like 100 times a day. Notice that it's running on CNN, not exactly the worst demographic you can imagine. There must be a reason that it's working. Well, there is.

Americans really are up to their eyeballs in debt. The average U.S. household carries more than $8,000 in credit card debt. Filings for personal bankruptcy have increased nearly 8 percent per year to well over a million and a half annually. This must be getting the attention of those folks who haven't yet reached critical mass.

Over half of our respondents say they have become more practical in their purchases. (See Figure 6.3.) Forty-five percent indicate they want to pay down debt; 39 percent say they want to decrease spending;

FIGURE 6.3 *Needs Take Precedence Over Wants as Shoppers Look to Decrease Debt*

	All	American Express & AMEX Blue	Master-Card	Visa	Discover
*In the last six months, have you made any of the following changes?**					
I have become more practical and realistic in my purchases.	51%	50%	52%	51%	47%
I have become less practical and more impulsive in my purchases.	5	5	4	5	5
I focus more on what I need rather than what I want.	60	58	61	61	57
I have become more conscious about food safety.	24	27	26	25	24
I am spending more time and money on decorating my home.	13	17	15	14	14
I worry more about political and national security issues.	26	28	28	28	27
I have reordered priorities in my daily life.	29	26	27	29	24
I have reordered priorities in my professional/ working life.	16	17	17	17	14
I am spending more time with my family.	31	28	31	31	29
I have not made any changes.	19	24	21	20	25
*Which of the following financial steps are you planning to take in the next three months?**					
Refinance home	5%	8%	6%	6%	6%
Pay down debt	45	49	53	51	47
Increase savings	36	40	39	39	36
Pay with cash more often	33	34	36	36	30
Buy stocks	9	18	11	10	12
Sell stocks	4	10	5	5	6
Decrease overall spending	39	42	43	41	39
None	22	21	20	21	24
Other	3	3	2	2	1

*Totals exceed 100 percent due to multiple answers
Source: STORES 2003 Consumer Credit Survey, conducted by BIGresearch.

and a third promise they will be using cash more frequently. This may be one place where BIGresearch predictions won't pan out. After all, these same folks say they intend to lose weight after New Years. But at least it's a sign.

If your customers are telling you they intend to be more practical, what should you do?

Here's a hint. Take, for example, appliance sales. How can you present the purchase of a new, more energy-efficient appliance as a practical alternative to keeping the old, inefficient, maintenance-prone

FIGURE 6.4 *Females Outpace Males in Debit Card Use*

Females Outpace Males in Debit Card Use

I use my debit card to buy . . .

Males   Females

	Males	Females
Clothing	45%	55%
Groceries	47%	53%
Health & beauty aids	46%	54%
Electronics/Furniture	47%	53%
Gasoline	46%	54%

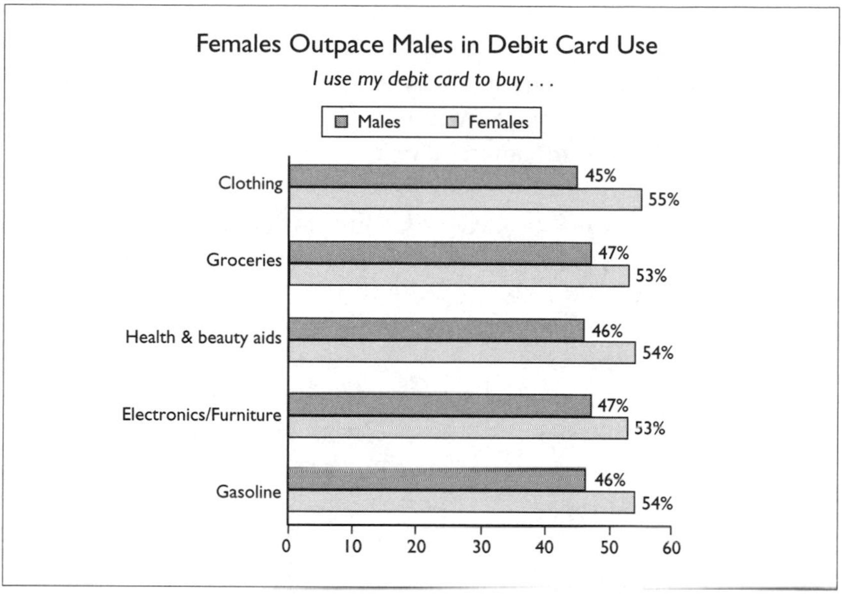

Source: STORES 2003 Consumer Credit Survey, conducted by BIGresearch.

clunker? Yeah, that's the ticket! Buying a new washer will save us money! We can spend our way to a more practical lifestyle!

In fairness, there really does seem to be a trend toward more practical paying, if not more practical spending, visible by the increasing use of the debit card. Debit card use is strongest among the 18- to 34-year old group. It is slightly more of a phenomenon as well. (See Figure 6.4.)

An *American Demographics* study, as reported in *Stores* magazine, showed that the average 21-year-old had $3,000 in credit card debt! Thirty-six percent of all consumers say they intend to increase savings. Among the 18–34 group, that number amounts to nearly half. Forty-four percent of the younger group say they also intend to decrease spending.

THE PRICE IS RIGHT

- Coupons? Who has time to cut coupons? Just lower the price! I will not buy if a coupon is required for a lower price.
+ Sales flyers
+ Price-match guarantee
+ Accepting competitors' coupons

- Retailers who jack up the prices so they can advertise a "sale" price
- Higher prices at the register than what was marked on the shelf
+ Free gift with purchase
- Price gouging by oil companies
+ Little sale signs mounted on or hanging from the shelf

Little sale signs hanging from the shelf—who would think that signage would be a big deal for shoppers? Obviously, signs help customers locate product, but they also educate in two ways: Signs tell us about price and quantity and, in the better stores, give us ideas about value in terms of cost per unit.

That signs also educate shoppers is much less obvious. Eric Anderson and Duncan Simester said it best (*Harvard Business Review*, September, 2003): " . . . retailers send signals to customers, telling them whether a given price is relatively high or low."

How do they do that? Is it on purpose? Can I do it, too? They do it with signs and pricing cues. They sometimes do it on purpose and, yes, you can do it, too!

Anderson and Simester refer to pricing cues that telegraph to the customer information about the value of the item. This is done in at least two important ways: by the price itself and by the percentage of prices that are labeled as sale prices.

It turns out that prices ending in "9" are more attractive to buyers. In one test, identical dresses were sold at three price levels: $34, $39, and $44. Anderson and Simester experimented with several versions of catalogs that were identical in all aspects except for price. What they discovered was that raising the price of the dress from $34 to $39 actually increased demand, while raising the price to $44 had no effect on demand for the dress.

Why? Customers apparently interpret a price ending in "9" as a sale price. When Anderson and Simester experimented with that idea, they discovered that customers offered merchandise with prices ending in $.99 were more likely, by about 8 percent, to purchase than customers offered prices in whole dollars.

One other way we cue signs about price and value is through the use of sale signs. When customers see a sale or clearance sign, they rely on the retailer's integrity and believe that the merchandise has been legitimately discounted. But be careful. Too many sale signs raise suspicion, and too many sale signs or too deep a discount may serve as a clue to the customer that the price may not really represent a bargain or, worse, that the quality of the merchandise is suspect.

Variable margin pricing is a method of taking advantage of the customer's pricing knowledge, or lack of it.

For each consumer, there are certain core prices that he or she is likely to know. Others, such as accessory items, are a near-complete mystery. In the newspaper, I found an ad for 24-ounce store-brand chocolate syrup for 99 cents. Is that really a deal? I haven't a clue, except for the banner above the section that advises me to "Stock up and Save." Since I trust this particular retailer, I assume this is a deal and I should buy several. Besides, a snipe next to the syrup reminds me to "add to ice cream for a sweet treat."

It is that zone of mystery that is the heart of variable margin pricing. I really don't know about the price of the chocolate syrup, nor about the going rate for the ice cream displayed next to it. The ice cream is not on sale but, hey, I've got all this syrup.

I was hoping to do this with hardware ads, but today is Wednesday and fishing in the paper yielded only this item of interest, "Sanderson Farms boneless, skinless chicken breasts $2.99/lb.," while at another store they are $2.59 a pound. Which of the two stores will enjoy a higher margin this week? It depends. It depends on what else the customer buys, if anything.

If the customers run in and cherry-pick the deals, there may not be a margin at all. But if the items are strategically placed near complementary items that might logically be purchased along with the chicken breasts, the decision will go to the better retailer, not necessarily to the retailer with the cheapest sale item.

Here's a quick quiz. What is the everyday price for boneless, skinless chicken breasts? You don't know, do you? And notice that one store had boneless, skinless chicken breasts, while the other had Sanderson Farms boneless, skinless chicken breasts, which are obviously worth more or, why would the grocer make a point of mentioning it? This is another price-value cue, only this one was delivered via weekly circular.

Since the price difference is so great between the two stores, when I really think this through, do you suppose I may begin to suspect that the cheapest breasts might be small or even old?

WRAP IT IN AN EXPERIENCE

This chapter was supposed to focus on *how* consumers want to be sold, but it may be worthwhile to think first about *what* consumers want to be sold. You do that by listening.

If you've never been in a Rent-A-Center store, you are missing retail heaven. This may not be the smoothest way to explain what they do, but in a nutshell, they rent furniture, appliances, and home electronics, including some pretty sophisticated PCs, to folks who for the most part don't have two nickels to rub together.

They rent this stuff by the week!

Customers pay what many would consider rather steep prices, and they pay for it every week. And if they don't pay—most do—a couple of nicely dressed, polite, young men in a shiny truck will knock on your door, roll out your fridge, your couch, your bed, and your widescreen TV, thank you for your business, and invite you to come to see them when you get caught up.

It seems bizarre, and in some ways it is, but Rent-A-Center was listening when people complained. The lower-income folks and folks who only need an apartment full of furniture for a short time seemed to get the short end of the stick when dealing with traditional furniture stores.

And Rent-A-Center listens when they select the goods they will be offering. Their customers want big-screen TVs, and they want speakers for their stereo that shout POWER! I know a little bit about audio equipment, and I can tell you the speakers I saw were huge but acoustically not all that good. But so what? This customer thinks that visually impressive definitely trumps frequency range and power.

Listen when the customer talks and let him or her tell you how, and what, he or she wants to be sold.

Someone was listening when the Penske Automotive Group built the *Scottsdale 101 Auto Collection,* called by *Men's Journal* a "high-end shopper's Paradise." It comes complete with 11 auto brands, each with its own showroom and a Starbucks-serving café to keep you comfortable while you shop. But the master's touch comes not from the aggregation, but from the recognition that each brand offers a distinct experience.

And play to the experience is exactly what they do! The Jaguar dealership features a clubroom that could have been lifted straight from an English polo club. At Land Rover, prospective owners are invited to take a spin on the off-road test track that was built out back. The Volvo crowd gets treated to a sleek Scandinavian-style showroom.

Experience. That's how people want to be sold. Unfortunately, they don't particularly want to pay for the experience. The future of retailing will not belong to price or quality but to those who can provide the most experience . . . efficiently!

AND THE WINNER IS?

The winner, or at least one of them, may be Starbucks. True, we don't often consider hospitality quite the same as retailing, yet you must admit they are at least kissing cousins. Starbucks listened when it first decided that customers would be willing to pay $4 for a fancy cup of coffee. I wasn't there, but my guess is they were as surprised as the rest of us, and only after the fact did they realize it was the experience they were selling!

Part of the Starbucks experience has always been the music, never too loud, never too sappy, always in tune with a cozy atmosphere offering respite from the office, traffic, and business. The folks at Starbucks noticed their customers, like the audience in a THX-equipped theatre, were listening. And so is born The Hear Music Coffeehouse, which is Starbucks' idea of how music retailing is supposed to be.

Researching the concept, Starbucks listed all the things about buying music that annoy and corporately said, "Don't do that." Likewise, they asked what delights customers about music and the experience of choosing it and corporately said, "Let's do more of that."

At Hear Music, you'll be able to select an entire album or a single track from a dozen albums and, in a matter of minutes, a friendly barista of boogie will hand over your custom CD complete with the title of your choice, disk, and jacket artwork, even the liner notes.

Look at the features of Hear Music and you practically have a list of what consumers tell us they want from a retail experience:

- Coffee, music, and wood (comfortable environment)
- Laid-back salespeople (no pressure selling)
- Suggestions, if you ask (knowledgeable salespeople)
- Database of 150,000 titles (wide selection)
- Your choice for about $1 per track (customization at value prices)

THE CUSTOMER HAS SPOKEN

The results are in, and there is little surprise. Give me knowledge-able, helpful salespeople but only when I want them. Make them easy to find and, if it's not too much trouble, have them also treat me nicely. Make things easy to find, give me a deal, and when I'm ready to leave, make it quick. And, by the way, checkout is your last opportunity to let me know that you really listen when customers talk.

For more information, visit http://www.whencustomerstalk.com.

7

ENGINEER THE EXPERIENCE

It's too easy to focus on product, price, packaging, and promotion and forget the service experience, but forget we do. We attempt to play for the buying emotion with price and glitzy packaging, while neglecting to work with the emotions, which cause customers to remember the experience fondly enough to come back. We slash prices until there is little or no margin and turn right around and offend our guests with rude employees, disastrous displays, dirty restrooms, and high-pressure sales tactics.

Simply said, customer service is the expression of your brand. Managing the brand is done in large part by managing the service experience.

So what do we know about designing the service experience? Here are a few important principles, some of which are the result of research done by the famous team of Chase and Dasu.

BRAND DEFINED

You can interpret the above heading two ways: (1) we're about to define what is a brand or (2) a product is defined by its brand.

A brand is an expectation. That's it. Nothing less, nothing more. It is a shortcut in the mind of the consumer. When consumers read or hear a product name, they immediately, and ofttimes subconsciously, conjure up an entire set of expectations that, if the brand is a good one, saves marketers time and money, thanks to the mental shortcut to consumers' minds.

If I say "Pepsi," you think what? Well, here's a small issue. Brands are highly individual. Marketers would like to own the same mental real estate in the mind of every consumer, but the truth is we each have a slightly different expectation, even when we are considering the same brand.

If I say "Pepsi," you may think youthful, popular, tastes good. If you say "Pepsi," the mental real estate Pepsi owns with me is sticky, not Coke, and Michael Jackson's hair is on fire. Obviously, I'm not a soda drinker, but I can tell you this—we sell a ton of Pepsi products at our restaurant, Sporty's!

When you already own mental real estate with your customers, marketing is more efficient. There is considerably less need to educate the market about your product's fundamentals. Marketers of strong brands can get straight to the offer, while new brands have to hoe a different row.

When we opened Sporty's, we had to run a whole campaign themed, "What's a Sporty's?" Our sign may have read Sporty's, a Casual Café, but the consumer read it as Sporty's, a sports bar. When given my 30-second new-member introduction at the local chamber of commerce, I chanted, "Sporty's is not a bar . . . it's a restaurant and a nice one at that! Meet me at Sporty's!"

Weeks after opening, we were still getting calls asking, "Can I bring my two sons there?" Or worse, the salesguy at Radio Shack on noticing my Sporty's shirt said, "How's everything at Sporty's?"

"Goin' great," I replied. "Have you been in?"

"I'm not that much of a drinker."

"What's that got to do with it?"

"Well, don't you just have beer and television?"

A brand is an expectation. It is mental real estate that you own in the mind of the consumer, and the real estate you own is different for every person who experiences your brand. How much would you pay for a shortcut into the hearts and minds of your customers?

I just read on InterBrand.com that the value of the Coca-Cola brand is somewhere in the neighborhood of $72.5 billion. That's billion with a *B*! Microsoft is worth $70.5 billion (per InterBrand.com). Enron and

MCI each weigh in at a big fat zero, which is testimony to the fact that it's entirely possible to lose brand equity in a heartbeat.

For the butcher, the baker, and the local electrician, there are also brand equities, as in "I wouldn't let anyone but Benno wire my house," which is a local version of "I'd walk a mile for a Camel" or even "I'd rather fight than switch!"

What is the value of your brand as a business, as a boss, or even as Dad?

BRAND VERSUS LOGO

The logo is what you see. The brand is what you think. Logo does not equal brand.

Too many retailers think about branding and head straight to the nearest graphic designer for ideas about how to illustrate their clever business name. Wrong! If the brand is strong enough, you don't even need a logo.

Logo stuff, if you stretch branding theory to the limits, can consist of sounds, sights, even smells.

Harley-Davidson tried to trademark the distinctive sound of a Harley. They lost, but only in the legal sense. Stand on my parking lot at Sporty's when the bikers are in town and tell me you can't tell the difference between the deep rumble of a pack of hogs and the quiet purr of a flight of Gold Wings.

Krispy Kreme Doughnuts recently came out with a drink flavored like a glazed doughnut. (Let me know if you get up the courage to taste one!) And what picture do you get if I sing, "Oh, I wish I was an Oscar Mayer wiener. That is what I'd really like to be . . ." At least mentally, I know you sang along with me. Now there's a tune as logo stuff.

A pin is dropping in slow motion across your television screen. That's logo stuff for Sprint, just as a swoosh on the side of a running shoe evokes images of Nike.

Employees are logo stuff. I don't mean that as coldly as it sounds. However you name it, employees serve as surrogates for your brand, and they must look and act in a manner that is congruent with the mental real estate that you want to own in the mind of the consumer.

ARTICULATING THE BRAND

What real estate do you want to own in the mind of the market? Do you want to be the low-price leader? Do you want to be known as the quality standard or be first in terms of innovation and style?

No matter what real estate you would like to own, you must first find out if it's available. Here's a marketing fact: No two organizations can own the exact same mental real estate. They can be close neighbors, but they can't own the same property. For men's clothing (remember, the numbers will change depending on the department or product), Kohl's and Sears are neighbors, while Kohl's and Macy's live in different parts of town.

Motivators for Buying Men's Clothing

	Kohl's	**Sears**	**Macy's**
Price	64.2%	75.1%	73.8%
Selection	53.2%	77.3%	83.7%
Location	38.2%	46.2%	53.0%
Quality	58.7%	66.3%	74.1%
Service	17.6%	18.6%	22.4%

Source: BIGresearch.

Based solely on the numbers, if you had never heard of these stores, where would you go if you needed a suit and had no time to shop? It's obvious that Macy's is the place. Good prices, best selection, better quality, and service. Just look at the numbers.

What could the position statements of the men's departments for each of these stores look like?

- Kohl's . . . men's clothing if you happen to be in the store
- Sears . . . men's clothing at a reasonable price
- Macy's . . . great selection of quality men's clothing

Having a brand and wanting a brand are two different things. By definition a brand is an expectation, so if consumers know you at all, you have a brand. The question then becomes, "Is the brand you have the brand you want?"

To build a powerful brand you need three tools:

1. A position that you can profitably fill
2. The ability to articulate your brand
3. A means of communicating your branding message

By extension, if there is a leadership crisis in America, it must include the leader's inability to communicate the "brand" to the troops. Unless the brand is effectively communicated to the troops as well as the public, it will never achieve its potential.

TAGLINES AND BRAND STATEMENTS

We're taking a bit of liberty with the science of branding when we talk as though the brand statement and the marketing slogan of the month are the same. A brand statement and marketing slogan are close enough to be cousins, however. It is the marketing slogan—the tagline—that does as good a job as any at telling the customer who you are.

The tagline advantage should be short and memorable, while at the same time communicating a ton of message in a few words. Taglines work just as well to focus employees as they do customers. A company with a memorable tagline constructed of a few powerful, image-provoking words will beat a multipage brand statement any day of the week!

Great taglines answer the question, "What do we do?" There's extra credit if it also tells for whom and why. Here are two excellent examples of hardworking taglines. The first belongs to Verizon: Can you hear me? Can you hear me now?

Two of the biggest problems in the cell phone industry are: coverage is often spotty, and so is the customer service. Many consumers believe that the rabbit warren of confusing rate plans is little more than a thin disguise for scamming the public. So Verizon says, We never stop working for you, which fairly shouts dependable service and "We're on your side!"

Xerox stakes their claim in three powerful words: The document company. Which of the three words do you think is the hardest working? The. They are not just a document company, but THE document company. In three words, Xerox lets you know if you need handling, storing, and duplicating of documents, Xerox is the one to call.

FedEx: The world on time. It pretty much says it all. FedEx does much of the work, because it is an established brand. Only the dead would not take the mental shortcut and fill in the blanks with thoughts of fast delivery and premium service. The remaining four words form the heart of the new message: We're worldwide and we get it there when you want it . . . on time.

If you don't have a heavyweight brand with a lot of equity, you may need a few extra words to do the job. If I said, "Sporty's, we've got your game," that might not give you a complete and accurate picture. So we work a little harder and say, "Sporty's: 18 big TVs . . . we've got your game." (That's an example; it's not our brand statement!)

How do you communicate the brand? One absolute necessity is a simple and clear brand statement that ordinary people can learn without effort and instantly understand. Wal-Mart: Always low prices, always. Got it? Lowe's: Improving home improvement. It pretty much says it all. Southwest Airlines: Freedom to move about the country. All of these taglines work hard and don't require a lot of words.

If you want to go the entire route, why not do what Levi Strauss & Company did when it moved training classes to art galleries, nightclubs, and other places where consumers might wear Levi's? Employees were outfitted with cameras and dispatched to capture examples of the brand being built, or abused, and to discover what the brand really meant in the eyes of the marketplace.

What could you do to more accurately articulate your brand?

PLAN ON PURPOSE

Failing to map out and plan the experience is the biggest service mistake we make. And too often when we do plan, we start from inside the store rather than outside.

In the hospitality industry, one great example is the new Red Lobster restaurants. From the moment you spy the building, you know you have come to the right place for seafood. Macaroni Grill also does a good job of starting the experience from the outside. Banana Republic makes a pretty good attempt. Most retailers' store exteriors offer little more than a bland, homogenous experience, if you can call it an experience at all.

While you are planning, it might be a good idea to include a few customers. Southwest Airlines is known to invite frequent flyers to assist in interviewing prospective flight attendants. Makes sense, as the customer ultimately has to live with the hiring decision.

An ad for Courtyard by Marriott—one of my favorites—reads: "Architects design most hotels. Road warriors designed ours." And it is surely one of the few hotels designed by guests.

The typical hotel room is a work of efficient layout but disastrous function. The entry lightswitch also works the floor lamp, so it is all or nothing. The faucet at the sink was a dime cheaper, but two inches shorter than it needed to be, so when you run the water, it dribbles along the side of the sink. And who is the malformed mess of a human being who can sit at the desk chair and not have the desk so high that typing on a Notebook doesn't look like you are attempting to slam dunk your Dell?

Of course, the worst design award goes to the committee in charge of the meeting rooms. Business meetings need real lights. Meeting rooms *are* used for more than cocktail parties, you know!

Courtyard got things pretty close to right for the business traveler. Comfortable rooms at a fair price, free use of a modest exercise facility, and a small pool. The hotels are built to human scale, unlike the monstrous convention hotels. Marriott asked the customer, and Marriott got it right.

To create a killer service experience, you have to consider every point of contact from Web site to Yellow Pages ad, from pole sign to shopping cart. Beyond managing the experience at every point of contact, it is critical that each point work together to present a unified, congruent experience of the brand.

MANAGE SURPRISE

We learned years ago the power of positive surprise. In our first restaurant, we struggled for the first four years until we discovered the power of positive surprise and named it Positively Outrageous Service. We found out that a small gesture that surprises and delights the customer has the incredible power to do three things.

First, a small surprise creates a halo effect that wraps around the business in such a way that on the next visit service may seem better than it really is. You could call it an afterglow effect: Wow me today, and tomorrow I will at least imagine that you still love me.

The second benefit of a small wow is that it creates a tendency toward reciprocity. In English that means when I do a little something for you, you feel psychologically compelled to do a (usually) big something for me. (For a complete discussion of the concept, see *Influence, the Psychology of Persuasion* by Robert Cialdini, Quill, 1998.) What is cool about reciprocity is the idea that a little something gets exchanged for a big something.

A few years ago, I happened to talk by phone with a client who mentioned that his daughter was big into competitive ice-skating. He mentioned the date of an important competition, and out of habit I entered the date into my contact management program, set an alarm for the big day, and, since the date was several months away, forgot about it.

But the computer didn't. On the appointed day, it signaled me to act. In my desk, there was an old postcard purchased at the Olympic Games in Los Angeles. I scribbled a message expressing hope that the competition had gone well, dropped the card in the mail, and forgot about it. Three days later the phone rang, "Got your card! Thought you'd like to know she came in second place. By the way, are you interested in speaking on . . ."

The cost? Thoughtfulness: zero. Postcard: 50 cents. Speaking engagement: priceless.

The third benefit of a positive surprise, or wow, is that it results in positive, compelling word of mouth. Since you were a kid, you've heard that the best advertising is positive word of mouth. Make someone say "Wow," and they have to talk about the experience. Here's one from an e-mail I received from Darlene Gavin of Domenic & Anthony, caterers to the elite in Boston:

> ". . . reports were forecasting two massive storm patterns that would drop 18–24 inches of snow with 30–40 mile per hour winds . . . (conditions) were reaching near blizzard conditions . . . so I left the shop two hours ahead of the catering truck to set up. Fearful that I would be working with a skeleton crew at best (road conditions were near impassable), I began formulating contingency plans for serving the meal. But one by one, my entire team of servers blew in the door—albeit dusted with snow.
>
> "The kitchen crew arrived to an unplowed loading area and shoveled a path for the catering truck without complaint. There seemed to be a camaraderie amongst everyone involved that we were going to do our best to get this wedding off the ground and make it the best day possible for this unfortunate couple.
>
> "Almost 80 percent of the guests arrived and the reception went off without a hitch. The third member of the Irish trio managed to show up just in time for the introductions. They started the dinner music with a whimsical version of 'Let It Snow, Let It Snow, Let It Snow,' which set a fun tone for the rest of the reception.
>
> "By 8:00 PM the truck was ready to head back to the shop. During the time we had been at the club, an additional half-foot of snow had fallen and the truck was stuck. Once again, everyone pulled together and shoveled and pushed until the truck was free . . . with a big cheer it headed on its snowy way.
>
> "The wait staff was sent home as soon as we were able to let them go and I stayed until the reception ended (so I could help with the) breakdown. I changed back into my warm clothes and boots and shoveled out my four-wheel-drive SUV.

"Most of the guests had departed when a very upset groom came barreling in the door. All of the parking in this location is on the street and two of the cars transporting the bridal party . . . the slightly tipsy parents of the groom, still in their formal-wear, were in the middle of the road with the best man trying to push the car out of the snow. I warned them to get out of the street, went for my shovel, and dug the cars out.

"I'm not even certain if the groom's parents realized who I was underneath my ski cap and parka . . . nor does it matter. While I shoveled, all were complaining about the weather conditions to me when (finally) I replied, 'Yes, but it could have been worse, your caterer may not have showed up!'"

Yeah, I'd call that Positively Outrageous Service! It was definitely a wow! And if it happened to you, you would definitely tell the world!

The expanded definition of Positively Outrageous Service reads like this:

- Random and unexpected
- Out of proportion to the circumstance
- Invites the customer to play
- Creates compelling, positive word of mouth
- The service story you can't wait to tell!

Manage surprise. Make it work for you. Turn ordinary service into Positively Outrageous Service!

Back to another e-mail to cement the point:

"I've been promoting the POS concept with our FBO (gas stations for airplanes) dealers as much as possible. I discussed it with our new dealer, Hap's Aerial Enterprises, in Sellersburg, Indiana, recently and he gave it a try. At a recent lunch he said, 'Hey, I tried that POS thing you have been telling me about and it worked!'

"I was so tickled I asked him for the details. He found a coupon for a pizza lunch for two and stuffed it into an envelope and wrote "You're a winner" on the outside. He gave it to the line-man and instructed him to give it to the next aircraft to arrive and tell the pilot that he's the 40th customer of the day.

"The lineman did as he was instructed with the next customer. A small twin-engine aircraft was the next to arrive and ordered ten gallons in each wing tank. The lineman handed the envelope to the pilot and told him he was a winner. The pilot was so happy that he changed his order to a top-off (fill-up) resulting in an increased sale $100 more than the original request.

"I asked our customer how much the increased sale had cost him and he said, 'Nothing except the effort.' He's now going to try some other off-the-wall ideas to keep the creative juices flowing.

"I have two other customers that I am buying your book for to 'infect' them with the POS virus." (Greg Miller, Air BP Aviation Services)

PLANNED SPONTANEITY

The guiding principle behind Positively Outrageous Service can be summed up in two words—unexpected wow. But how do you plan spontaneity?

You don't plan how to wow as much as you plan *that* you wow. Okay, you can fudge by giving a few pointers. At Sporty's, we sell a dessert called The Big Dog. It has a foundation of a custom-baked iced brownie, a pile of ice cream, a mountain of whipped cream, a handful of cherries, a drizzle of chocolate, and a few long-handled spoons arranged around the large silver dog dish that we serve it in (Pepto Bismol not included).

Order The Big Dog and it will be delivered to your table to the strains of "Who let the dogs out?" From around the restaurant, servers, cooks, managers, and familiar guests chant "Who? Who? Who Who?" as a smiling server parades from table to table showing the monster dessert until it finally lands in front of its new owner.

In other words, we've engineered a bit of planned surprise. Overall, it is better to simply set the stage and then stand back and let well-hired team members deliver their lines impromptu.

CELEBRATE POS

When faced with an opportunity to step out of the box and deliver a solid dose of Positively Outrageous Service, is the employee thinking about the customer or the company? Either response is dead wrong. When the wow opportunity arises, most employees are thinking about one thing only—themselves. Face-to-face with a customer or guest who definitely qualifies for a touch of POS, the employee's thoughts are a mishmash of "Will this work? Does it cost too much? What if they don't appreciate it?" In a single sentence, the employee wants to know one thing: "If I do this, will I get killed by the boss?"

There are only two things necessary to encourage POS in your operation, assuming you have already had the good sense to hire a team of Service Naturals. You have to model POS and celebrate POS. Modeling POS is simple. The boss goes first.

With the boss as an example, it's much easier to trust that a little creativity and spontaneity will be appreciated rather than quashed. At Sporty's, part of our décor includes a basketball backboard and hoop mounted high in our main dining area. To identify waiting guests, we give each party a different colored soft basketball.

Hmmm! Basketballs and backboards. Maybe we ought to use them. Hey! Why not let customers shoot for Brownie Bites? A great idea! But to our servers, shooting baskets in the middle of the dining room seemed a bit radical and, even though we talked about it, there wasn't exactly a rush to actually do it.

Imagine what your mother would say: "Go ahead. Jump on the couch all you want because when you get older, I'm coming to your house and shooting baskets in the dining room! See how you'll like that!" So I started the ball rolling, metaphorically speaking.

"I see you ordered ten macho hot wings. You're never going to be able to eat all ten."

"Sure I will. I'm hungry and I eat even more at Hooters."

"Yes, but that's at Hooters. You're at Sporty's and our wings are huge."

"No problem."

"Well, if you can eat all ten without help, I'll let you shoot two to make one for a Brownie Bite. Ask your server to call me if you don't wimp out."

And that's how a mondo-bizarro practice was born, but only because the boss went first.

PUT THE CUSTOMER FIRST

Above all, for a service experience to be truly great, you must be willing to value people over policy. One post-Christmas Sunday, we ventured into the big city to return a pair of jeans that did not fit. We had two problems. First, the store had a policy that required a sales receipt that we did not have; we had the bag but not the receipt. Second, all we wanted to do was exchange the pair we had for an identical pair in a different size.

That should have been simple, right? Well, wrongo rio! We began by approaching a cashier, after waiting in her slow-moving line for the better part of 20 minutes, only to be told, "Sorry, you have to take it over there."

"Over there" was somewhere beyond a serpentine line that had to have 50 frustrated shoppers waiting for a single clerk. I'm a good sport, but once in the new line for nearly ten minutes, we turned a corner only to be confronted by a sign that read, "No returns or exchanges without the original receipt."

"Buns, do you know anyone who wears this size?" I held up the jeans with the expression that added a huge implied, "Please." She didn't, but looked over my shoulder at the remaining mile of frustrated people and said, "Salvation Army?" A done deal! And we were done with that store forever. They had clearly demonstrated that policy was more important than people, at least to them.

MORE FOR DEFINITION

If you take the definition for POS—random and unexpected; out of proportion to the circumstance; invites the customer to play; and creates compelling, positive word of mouth—and change the circumstances 180 degrees, you will discover that the definition for the best service you have ever had is also the definition for the worst service you've ever had. Think about it. Wasn't the worst service you ever had random and unexpected, out of proportion to the circumstance? Were you not highly involved, and did it not create compelling, although negative, word of mouth?

Just as we are compelled to tell others when we have been the recipient of a positive surprise, we are likewise compelled to tell the world when the surprise is a negative.

ENGAGE THE CUSTOMER

It makes service seem faster and waiting fast. The truth is it doesn't matter how long the customer waits. It only matters how the customer feels about the wait.

Have you ever waited for the Matterhorn at Disneyland? It's normally a long, boring wait. How about the wait for ET at Universal? That wait is almost better than the ride! At the Olive Garden, when they are sampling hot bread sticks, I can wait forever. The wait is only as long as it feels.

Invite me to linger. Once you have me inside, convince me to stay. The best example I've seen is the Bose factory outlet stores. If you haven't visited one, I promise it's worth the drive as well as the wait. The featured attraction is a demonstration of Bose audio equipment in the cozy in-store theater. The show is interesting and informative, and there are a few surprises that get the audience talking. It's fun, it's free, and it's over almost as soon as it begins.

It's not the wait. It's how you feel about the wait.

One of the best ways to involve the customer is through humor and fun. Be careful! Not everyone is ready to play, and not every circumstance lends itself to humor. But many do, and smart operators understand how to take advantage of a customer who is "in fun" (ready to play). Minutes ago, I took a writing break and picked up the latest issue of *Fast Company*. Glued between the pages was what looked like an instruction card, similar to what you expect to find in an airline seat-back pocket.

The card was printed on heavy stock in official-looking type in "emergency red" color. Just as on the airlines, the copy was in English with a Spanish translation and the admonishment: PLEASE DO NOT REMOVE FROM MAGAZINE! It was an ad for Virgin Atlantic, giving instructions for using the "Tension Escape Routes." Just a touch of fun to get your attention.

Bad Stuff First, Good Stuff Last

Chase and Dasu discovered that the final moments of a single experience shape a customer's feelings about the entire experience. What do smart operators do? They get things like waiting and form completion out of the way early in the process and design the service experience to end with something pleasant. It could be a free dessert or an escort to your car or even handing you the keys to your new car while pointing out that the fuel tank is full. What if a fine-dining restaurant notified the valet at the same time it processed your credit card, so there would be no unpleasant waiting for your car to be exhumed from deep in the parking lot?

Serve the Servers

This is a favorite Southwest Airlines story. It's not a tearjerker. It's not the usual SWA flamboyant. It's just a simple story of passion for service.

SWA cofounderHerb Kelleher was known for working Black Wednesday, the busiest of all flying days, the day before Thanksgiving. Herb achieved near legendary status for showing up at a Southwest Airlines hub and working a full shift as a baggage handler, a rough, tough, grueling job made all the more difficult by full airplanes, rush Christmas packages, and often downright miserable weather.

Nice story, but that's not the one I have in mind, because working a shift or two at the plant or in the mine or wherever can be nothing more than a bit of internal theater, something gleaned from the latest management book. No, the story I want to share exists as lore taken from the inside of SWA. It has been repeated so many times that, like playing the whisper game at a party, no doubt I have the details wrong. But the concept is dead on. This one is pure Herb Kelleher, whose initials must surely be P.O.S.

The day had been long and arduous with full airplanes, weather down to minimums, and passengers who had gotten crankier and crankier as the SWA jet fell further and further behind schedule. It was not a happy day for traveling and, thanks to weather and traffic delays, that went double for a crew pushing the legal flying-time limits.

The last leg of the day was a flight from New Orleans to Houston. Beside the fatigue of a long day and a ride made worse by intermittent turbulence, the surface winds were out of the north at 15 knots with gusts to 24, making a straight-in landing out of the question. Instead, the hulking B-737 crossed the Daisetta navigation aid at 10,000 feet and prepared to circle completely around the airport some 60 or so miles away for a landing to the northeast.

For this leg, it was the first officer's turn to fly. So the captain took to the mic and advised the sleepy passengers and his exhausted cabin crew that he expected to be at the gate at approximately 1:15 AM.

When the mains touched gently on Houston Hobby's 7,602-foot-long runway 4, the flight got its first break of the day. If you're good, a landing to the northeast in Houston puts you right in line for a high-speed turnoff and almost direct to the ramp. Tired or not, SWA pilots are on their game and, in at least this respect, this night would be like any other.

The crew offered the obligatory, "Thanks for flying, good night" routine and began hauling their roll-aboards from nooks and crannies to begin the long trek to the terminal, wondering how they would get to their hotel at this late hour. A taxi would do it. A couple of bucks each and, assuming they could find a taxi, they would be head-to-pillow just after 2 AM.

Outside the baggage area, instead of a cab they saw a long black automobile sliding smoothly along the curb. Somebody must really rate to have a car and driver at this hour of the night, they thought. The black auto continued forward and stopped in front of the bedraggled crew. The trunk popped open and a tall, older gentleman, who in the light from the dome light looked remarkably like Herb Kelleher, stepped onto the pavement.

"Good morning," called a cheerful voice, still ragged from too many years and cigarettes. He called most of the crew by name and that sealed the deal. Only the real Herb Kelleher could do that, in spite of having a company roster pushing well beyond 30,000! "I saw that your plane was a little behind and thought you might like a ride."

That's how you serve the servers.

Segment Pleasure, Combine Pain

Perhaps the most interesting of Chase and Dasu's discoveries is that a transaction will seem to be more pleasant if unpleasant portions are concentrated into a single period, while pleasant portions of the experience are scattered throughout the transaction. What if Disney could put all of the waiting right at the beginning and design your final attraction to deposit you at the end right next to your car? Well, that would be a killer!

Diffuse Disappointment

When customers are disappointed, they also talk—but probably not to you. They will tell their friends and any stranger who will hold still to listen. Some disappointed customers will get in your face; many will simply go away.

If you want to diffuse disappointment, you have to search it out. On my desk is a comment card for Sporty's from a woman who wrote, "I was shocked to be charged for Ranch dressing . . . I do not eat Caesar." I haven't a clue what she is talking about, other than apparently she was charged for something she thought should have been included in the price. She rated our atmosphere a perfect 10. And even with her shock over something as small as salad dressing, she rated the service an 8. In other words, she liked us. Allow me to translate: "I really want to remain your customer, but you've got to fix this."

The only sensible attitude to have with disappointed customers is this: If you aren't happy, we aren't happy. The best way to diffuse disappointment is to share it with the customer.

"Ma'am, I'm shocked too. We should never have charged you for your choice of dressing. If that had happened to me, I might have been more than shocked. I would have been mad as the dickens! No doubt I missed something in our training. I'll correct that immediately. Please accept my apology and bring this letter to Sporty's for a salad of your choice on us!"

In the first week that we had opened Sporty's, one of our young customers wore a Sporty's T-shirt to school. Her shirt read simply, "Meet me at Sporty's." Her teacher, assuming that Sporty's was a sleazoid beer bar, demanded that the little girl go home and change her shirt.

We could have been indignant. We could have complained to her principal. We could have ignored her action entirely. Instead, we opted to diffuse her disallusion. We took menus and a voucher for her to sample our service at no cost. And we made a friend. Yesterday, I was called to a table of eight teachers. Guess who was their leader? The same woman who had assumed we weren't an appropriate place for children! She wanted to introduce herself and her friends, stating proudly, "This is my third visit!"

Say Yes

In hospitality, there are two things that separate the amateur from the seasoned pro. The amateur sees the big things; the pro sees the smallest details. And the amateur plays defense, while the pro plays offense. While the amateur is creating policies and employing barriers and technology to keep the customer from getting too close to the product, the pro is looking for ways to put the customer and product together. The simple premise is this: If the product is a quality product and the price is right, the sale is nearly a done deal if you can get trial.

If you are in business, you know that never a week goes by that some charity or civic organization doesn't ask for you to sponsor this event or take an ad in its so-called fabulous program. Should you say yes? Well, maybe, but definitely not unless your participation results in trial.

What can you do to encourage customers? How can you get them in intimate touch with your product and let them get their hands on it without hurry or undue restriction? Encouraging trial is just one way of saying yes to your customers. Essentially, all business is about problem solving. When a chef buys a food processor, he or she doesn't need another appliance but only the need for chopped carrots or pureed pear cactus. When a soccer mom shops for a minivan, she doesn't need another car in the driveway—she needs reliable, safe transportation for kids, pets, and groceries.

When customers make requests, they are saying, "Here is a problem. Can you help me solve it?"

Great service organizations actively seek to identify customer problems and devise ways to solve them that are better, cheaper, and faster than the solutions offered by the competition. Nordstrom is terrific about service. Their customers told us, and they tend to tell their friends as well. Enter Nordstrom with a problem and, so long as you are willing to pay for it and wait for it, you can count on having one less problem to solve.

The stories are legendary. A woman returns a set of tires to Nordstrom, where they are cheerfully exchanged. It's interesting to note that Nordstrom doesn't sell tires! (I assume this story is true. It is definitely an urban legend.) Another woman returns to the Nordstrom shoe department, complaining that the new, haute couture shoes do not fit properly. The alert salesperson notices that she has the shoes on the wrong feet! What did he do? He apologized and offered to make an immediate adjustment. Taking the shoes to the stock room, he made a great deal of banging noise before returning the "adjusted" shoes, turning a complaint into loyalty.

How are you saying no to your customers? How can you turn that no into a yes?

PUT THE CUSTOMER IN CONTROL . . .

. . . it makes them happy!

This principle explains the popularity of self-checkout. Coupled with the fact that 35 percent of our surveyed customers reported that rude/unfriendly/condescending clerks and salespersons are a problem, is, no doubt, the reason many shoppers are happy to avoid personal contact whenever possible.

Another reason for putting a customer in control is the customer. A former Disney exec, Jon Snoddy, was quoted in *FastCompany* as saying,

"There was a generation of people out there who . . . had lived their entire lives with a game plugged into their TVs . . . that has to change the way adults view entertainment. When you're playing a video game, you're in control. I think that has to affect people. It makes them demand a role in their own entertainment."

Today in the era of shopping as entertainment, being in control may be more important than ever.

Numerous restaurant operations and nearly every bank and service station have taken advantage of customers willing to take control of their transactions. It isn't a matter of lower prices. Many ATMs charge a hefty premium for their use. And gas prices? Who knows what they would be without pay-at-the-pump?

Self-serve does not really equate to "cheap" so much as it means "my way on my time."

What can you do to give your customers more control over the buying experience?

Make Customers Feel Important

There is a huge difference between appreciation and payoff. It is appreciation when the customer benefits; it's a payoff when a third party benefits. Customers love to be appreciated, and the easiest way to do that is to remember them.

Last night, we drove over the hill to the OST (Old Spanish Trail) Café in Bandera. We hadn't been there in quite a while and were missing the taste of good Tex-Mex food and the flavor of small-town Old West hospitality. Not five feet inside the door, we were greeted by a waitress who took one look at me, smiled, and said, "I know, burrito supreme, drowning in chili, smothered in cheese, and camouflaged with jalapenos. Oh, and one iced tea, the size of a house." She remembered. I felt plenty important.

There are plenty of ways to make customers feel important. You can ask their opinion, treat them to special hours, or offer them exclusive services. You can even make them privy to insider information.

If you are a regular at Tuesday Morning, you get invited to sales a day ahead of the general public. Business members are free to shop Sam's Club earlier than the general public. Several airlines offer free upgrades to first class frequent flyers, and VIP visitors are often invited for behind-the-scenes tours at venues from film studios to manufacturing plants. Pump enough quarters into the slot machines in Las Vegas, and suddenly your room rate is lowered—often to zero—you find yourself eating free at the buffet, and otherwise being pampered like the royalty you are.

What can you do to make your customers feel important? Somewhere in the paragraph above is an idea or two that will work for you.

HOW YA DOIN'?

If you are close to a computer, hop on the Internet and check out http://www.theacsi.com. What you will be looking at is the American Customer Service Index. If you work for one of the big boys, you'll see your score listed on the Web and know in a heartbeat how you fare in comparison to the competition. If you aren't playing in the big leagues, the site will show you who you want to emulate.

Be careful. Not all of the top dogs are doing a great job. If you copy the mediocre, the best results you can expect will be—mediocre!

Looking at the fast-food (QSR—Quick Service Restaurant) segment for the first quarter of 2004, we see what I would call some rather disappointing results. The baseline is only 69 percent (based on 100 points).

Baseline	69%
All Others	73%
Little Caesar	72%
Wendy's	72%
Pizza Hut	69%
Domino's	67%
KFC	67%
Burger King	66%
Taco Bell	66%
McDonald's	63%

"All others" are doing better than any of the top eight U.S. fast feeders. If you are in the that category, it may be a good idea to avoid following the big players too closely!

HIRE SERVICE NATURALS

Service stinks, service is sorry, service has gone straight down the drain. And I know why. There are three reasons: miscast employees, uncertain management, and antagonistic systems. All have come together in a perfect storm of incompetence that has left consumers thinking three thoughts of their own: price, price, and price.

But it doesn't have to be this way. Our research says that customers will pay more (not a lot), drive further (a lot further), and wait longer, if they think that there is an outside chance they will be waited on by a friendly, knowledgeable service person. They're even willing to take some of the blame for poor service. Our survey of 10,000 consumers cited rude customers as the fourth leading cause of stinky service!

Let's take a closer look at the three big, bad causes of stinky service.

We Hire People We Don't Want for Jobs They Don't Want

Culprit number one: miscast employees. A huge number of under-performing employees are working in jobs that simply do not fit either their talent or temperament. Simply put, never try to teach a pig to sing. It wastes your time and it irritates the pig!

We worked with 18 top corporate managers in a small study to determine what a quality service person might look like. We asked managers to participate in a brief survey to create the psychological profile of the ideal service person for a specific job in their company. We then asked them to identify their best service persons, which we, in turn, profiled and used to create a composite profile of a winning employee as defined by the boss.

Just for grins, we profiled the worst service employees in each of our participating companies as well. (We didn't call them losers, merely, strugglers.)

It was no surprise. The winning employees had a profile completely different from the strugglers. Much to our surprise, we discovered that the composite profile of the best servers did not in any way resemble the profile created by the boss! In simple terms, most bosses wouldn't recognize a great hire if one fell on them!

Let's back up for a second. Our 10,000 consumers mentioned rude customers as a major cause of poor service. How can this be? Why would customers blame themselves for crummy service? Well, it turns out they didn't exactly blame themselves, they blamed "the other guy." You see, customers aren't customers full-time. At work, they sit on the other side of the aisle! But how do we explain this? If nearly everyone complains about poor service, who is left to actually *deliver* poor service?

The answer is this: Rarely is poor service either intentional or recognized as being poor service by the person doing the serving.

Finding number two: For even the worst performers, there is likely to be a job in which they could be successful. It's too bad so few have found their niche. Nobody wants to look stupid. Nobody ever says, "I can't wait to get to work. I am such an idiot in that job!" Think about it. Your poorest performers are the same folks most likely to show up late or perhaps not show up at all. But, trust me, the employee you'd like to duct-tape to the floor could be just perfect somewhere else!

The challenge is to get the right people in and the people who are right for someplace else . . . out!

If the Boss Is Lost . . .

Culprit number two: uncertain leadership. Quick! What is your mission statement? Don't go digging out the stupid wallet card the consultant/change agent had printed for you. Just stand up and belt out that mission. And while you are bellowing, give us a chorus of core values. Can't do it, can you?

The team will usually follow where the boss decides to lead, so it's mighty helpful if the boss knows where this train is going. When you aren't certain of your destination, most any direction will do. The most boring function of leadership is hammering out those values, mission, and vision statements. It's too bad they are also among the most important things we can do. They are fundamental.

Leadership must behave in a way that is 100 percent congruent with the values, mission, and vision. If not, a new set of values, mission, and vision will be created de facto.

It's Not the Stupid Worker!

Culprit number three: antagonistic systems. Demming was right. It's not the stupid worker; it's the stupid work! Antagonistic systems are policies and procedures that actually work against the probability of good customer service.

We are so afraid that an employee is going to miscount the change, mess up the inventory, or make a decision that's going to cost a dime that we have dumbed down jobs in an attempt to make them idiotproof. When you make jobs idiotproof, should you be surprised to discover that only idiots can stand to work them?

When you run employees and customers against stupid rules, you frustrate employees and send customers scurrying to businesses with more flexibility. Visit the nearest fast-food restaurant and ask for a large cup of ice water. You will find yourself face-to-face with employees looking very much like deer caught in the headlights. They're likely to offer you several of their small courtesy cups, or they may offer to run a garden hose to your table, but they won't give you a large cup! Why? Because to prevent theft, the large cups are counted. For every large cup missing, there should be a large drink sale recorded on the cash register. It's not the stupid worker. It's the stupid work!

Everywhere you will find policies that stand in the way of good service. Show up early for your flight, and you may see a half-empty plane depart the gate while the flight you are on is overbooked. The airline would rather send a plane out with unsold seats than risk the integrity of their policy to charge a penalty for changing a reservation. It's not the stupid worker.

This afternoon we picked up a parcel at the local post office. It was one of those "as seen on TV specials," and Buns began to recount her ordering experience saying, "The order taker must have had a three-page script! Every time I would refuse one offer, she would skip to the next paragraph: "We have a special offer today . . ." "No, thank you." "Well, because you ordered our premium model . . ." "No, thank you." "As our way of saying thank you, you can choose any three magazines from the foll . . ." "No, thank you!"

When I asked Buns why she didn't ask the order taker to stop, she said: "It was her job, and you know all calls may be monitored. Well, I just didn't want her to get a demerit or something for not making it all the way through the script . . . but I won't order through them again."

Whose fault was the unhappy service? Not the worker; it was the antagonistic system that made good service impossible.

What systems are at work at your place making great service improbable, if not absolutely impossible? Is the return policy too restrictive? Are employees graded on speed but not rewarded for friendliness? Are there too few on staff to keep the store clean and well merchandised while still being available to assist customers?

It's not the stupid worker. It's the stupid work.

So, what will we do? Probably nothing! We'll remain in our comfort zone, calmed by conventional wisdom—you can't get good help, the schools don't teach kids to count, parents have given up teaching values—and watch the pennies and the dollars will follow.

Fine. If you've come this far without being a service fanatic, perhaps your luck will hold. But, one fine morning you may watch a new competitor move onto your turf and this one will be different—it will hire hard and fire easy. The new business will be fully focused on its values, mission, and vision, and it will go to any lengths to stamp out stupid policies. Until then, you are safe.

For a Song

This one is definitely a bit unairlinelike, but it's true. Flight attendants for Delta's new low-cost carrier, Song, have been given four tickets each to give to passengers who are "nice to one another." For a limited time, passengers caught in the act of being nice may find themselves "ticketed." Song CEO John Selvaggio said, "We always give away product when people have problems. I'd love to see what happens when you give away a ticket for somebody doing something good."

Look at This

If you can see this one, you don't need it. Posh restaurants, such as Bacchanalia in Atlanta, have begun serving a selection of reading glasses and penlights to their aging boomer guests who may have left their "cheaters" in the car or at home on the dresser. Older guests who are noticed having difficulty with the dim lighting or the fine print are discretely offered assistance. What does it cost? Practically nothing and, boy, does it generate positive buzz!

Make It Right

In great service operations, the policy is this: "We'll do whatever it takes to make things right when things go wrong."

Customers understand that employees are human, things happen, and sometimes things go wrong. What they don't understand is when things go wrong and business hides its hand. Think about Microsoft. Years ago, it discovered a glitch in Windows that could cause an absolute miniscule number of calculations to yield erroneous results. Even though it was suggested that the vast majority of users would never in a zillion years encounter the problem, Microsoft stepped up to the plate and made it right.

Contrast that with an edition of *60 Minutes* more than a decade ago, when Mike Wallace ambushed the then-CEO of Wal-Mart with footage of child laborers producing products Wal-Mart made in third world countries but marketed at home as made in America. I saw the program and had no doubt that the executive was truly surprised and maybe embarrassed. Had he said, "I can't believe this is true, but we'll investigate and get back to you with the facts," I don't think anyone watching would have thought twice about the incident. In the bonehead public relations goof of the century, a Wal-Mart executive, who had been watching off-camera, called off the interview, all of which was captured on tape. And Wal-Mart, which I know to be a highly ethical corporation, looked instead like corporate slime.

Complaints and challenges often represent your biggest opportunity to build loyalty and credibility.

And there are three things we know about complaints and complainers. First, complainers are taking the hard route in an effort to tell us what we probably should have already known. In a sense, complainers are saying, "I really want to be your customer but you really need to fix this!" It's much, much easier to tell your hairdresser or the garden club than to confront a defensive store manager or clerk.

Second, we've discovered that when asked what we must do to make things right, most of the time customers will ask for less than you would have settled for after negotiation. That's right. The cheapest way to resolve a complaint is often a matter of saying, "I'm sorry. What can we do to make things right?" It was one of those things you rip from a magazine and drop into a file thinking you may use it someday. (I'm telling you this, because I make no claim for either age or accuracy. It makes the point that as retailers we can be awfully hard on ourselves and may be scared away from doing what is right, simply because we're afraid of the cost.)

MasterCard ran a survey in 1992 in *Restaurants & Institutions* magazine, and the results, I thought, were remarkable. Asked if it was okay to change an order after it had been sent to the kitchen, over half of the restaurant operators surveyed said to do so was just fine. Less than a quarter of diners thought doing so would be okay. Nearly 70 percent of the operators felt it was fine to substitute an item on the menu, but less than half of the diners thought it could be done. Amazing!

And finally, the third thing we know about complaints and complainers is that customers who have never had a reason to complain are not as loyal as customers who have had a complaint that was successfully resolved. Read that again, please. This is so powerful, it's almost worth screwing something up just so you can fix it!

Deliver Status

Last night, I approached a birthday party in our 911 theme dining area (décor à la police, fire, and EMS). "Hi, folks! My name is Scott. I'm one of the owners, and I just wanted to make sure you're having a great time. I'm having dinner right over there, and if there is anything Brandy can't do to make you comfortable, I'll be happy to take care of it personally."

A short while later, I glanced over and noticed a member of the party attempting to change channels on one of the televisions in the room. I grabbed a remote control, presented it to the struggling guest, and said, "Ma'am, this is America. You're at Sporty's, and you can watch anything you want . . . except maybe Jerry Springer. And you, ma'am, are in charge of this delicate operation." With that, I left the happy crowd.

When the group called it an evening, four of the dozen made a point of finding me to tell me they appreciated getting attention from the owner. Now, I'm no one special, and, to be candid, I think sometimes when folks meet me in person I'm a bit of a disappointment. But at Sporty's, I'm the owner and people love to think that the boss is personally watching over their experience. Imagine how that whole transaction would have been received had I not begun by saying, "My name is Scott. I'm one of the owners."

Frequent-flyer or frequent-buyer programs that reward customer loyalty with upgrades, special services, or prices are other ways of making customers feel important. Entertaining clients is what keeps many restaurants and, no doubt, a host of golf courses in the black.

Without golf or game tickets or even frequent-buyer programs, what can you do to make the customer feel important?

Go First

Moments before speaking to an audience of 600 in St. Louis, I decided that a quick walk in the cool air of an early fall evening would be just the thing to shake off the grogginess of a full day of flying, meetings, and poor eating.

"Hey! I know you!" It was, I learned, the general manager of this luxury hotel. This guy was pretty, real pretty, wearing a fancy suit with flapper shoes, silk socks, and a tie arranged just so. His nails had been trimmed and polished causing me to hide mine deep in the pockets of my Dockers.

"You're the Positively Outrageous Service guy. What are you doing in my hotel?"

"I'm speaking to the group in the main ballroom in a few minutes. I'm going for a breath of fresh air before I go to work."

"May I join you?" I was surprised to be asked by Mr. Pretty.

I nodded and headed into the parking lot, turning left to walk counterclockwise around the hotel within sight of the runways at Lambert Field. We hadn't walked 100 yards before I noticed a piece of paper directly in my path. It was paper on a parking lot, and I did what I always do: without breaking stride, I bent and scooped it into my hand.

Mr. Pretty shot me a puzzled look but said nothing.

A bit further, another piece of trash showed up on radar. Again it was directly in front of me, and again I scooped it up without hesitation. Mr. Pretty shot another look, this one more puzzled than the last.

We walked another two or so minutes, talking about nothing in particular, when a final opportunity appeared on the horizon, only this time it was unquestionably aimed at Mr. Pretty. He came to a screeching halt, looked at the paper on the ground, and looked at the paper in my hand. He looked again at the paper on the lot and back again at the paper in my hand. I'm thinking, "Come on, pal! It's a little bending motion! You can do this!"

Mr. Pretty looked again at the paper on the lot and then to my hand. His expression telegraphed that he had made a decision. He took the paper from my hand, tossed it onto the lot, and explained, saying, "Don't worry. I have people to come out and clean this up." Is there a chance that Positively Outrageous Service will find a home at this hotel? Not a prayer!

If the boss doesn't go first, nobody goes.

One Last, Sickening Example

This was just what I wanted hear! The instant I walked through the door, one of our servers rushed to tell me the bad news. Two of our regular guests, who happen to be our server's neighbors, had eaten at Sporty's and soon after became violently ill. Food poisoning, they thought, and, without more information, I could only agree as my own stomach began to churn at what that kind of gossip would do to our fledgling enterprise.

"Please find out what they ate and ask them to call me. I want to know, and I want to make it right," was all I could think to say at the moment.

The following morning, on Sunday, my phone rang. (We post our personal number right on the menu, so if there is an unresolved issue, customers can talk straight to the guy who signed the loan application.)

"Good morning! This is Scott."

"Mr. Gross, you don't know me. But my wife and I and her parents were in your establishment last evening and, although I seem to be just fine, the others are all quite ill. I'm not calling to ask for anything, but I thought you would want to know."

I did want to know, sort of. If it was our fault, we would get right to the bottom before anyone else was hurt. But golly, as if opening a new restaurant wasn't hard enough . . . I ran through the list of possibilities and was completely stumped. The incubation time was a bit short but still within the realm of possibility. The real puzzlement was that they did not all eat something in common. Maybe it was an environmental thing like the AC or the water or who knows what.

I asked for his contact information, promised I would inspect the restaurant immediately and call him back with the results, and insisted that he accept dinner and drinks for four on the house. Then I did the unthinkable. I called the health inspector at home (on a weekend) to report the problem and ask for help. We talked at length by cell phone, and, like me, she was puzzled.

"Scott, I really don't think it's you. But you're right, two different parties . . . maybe it's more than mere coincidence. Please ask your customers to call my office in the morning, and I'll take their report. By the way, there is a vicious virus spreading through the area. The hospital did five spinal taps yesterday alone. They may have just been exposed at the same time."

I called our guest to let him know the current thinking and immediately mailed a letter good for dinner and drinks for four. Two days passed. Buns and I left town on business, but the idea that a foodborne illness would be pinned on the new restaurant in town was never far from mind. On the third day, the phone rang and a familiar voice said, "Mr. Gross? This is . . ." Here it comes. I knew it. The great holdup, the you'll-be-hearing-from-my-attorney routine. I held my breath as the voice continued.

"I went to the health department, as you suggested, and while we were there I happened to recall one other thing I failed to mention."

Look out, Elizabeth. Here comes the big one! I clutched my wallet like Fred Sanford would clutch his chest.

"We remembered that we had all eaten at a Mexican restaurant in our neighborhood where we all had a serving of guacamole. It turns out that at least eight others had the same thing and called the health department. It wasn't Sporty's at all. I really don't think I can accept your kind offer to dinner. Besides, when I got off the phone after our last conversation, I told my wife, 'He sounds like a real nice guy. He really listened.'"

Ladies and gentlemen, I rest my case.

8

RETAILERS AND SERVICE PROVIDERS WHO GET IT RIGHT

We asked. Customers talked. They told us in no uncertain terms what it takes to make them happy. Our first thought was to present a consumer's top-ten list, but when we looked at the numbers, well, it just didn't take ten things to be successful in the eyes of the consumer. Hit it big with the following list, and your customers will be more than happy. They'll be thrilled!

The list was generated by analyzing the responses of nearly 9,000 typical consumers. Consumers were asked to write in their answer to this question: "What things do you most like or dislike about a shopping experience?" There were no forced responses. In other words, there was not a list of answers from which to choose. Survey participants were asked to write in the answer of their choice. They were given a nearly unlimited amount of time and space for their answer. They were free to list as many issues as they wished.

The responses were analyzed by the Clusterizer, and human judgments were made to note that such responses as "I like fast checkout" were equivalent to "I don't like to wait in line to checkout" or "Slow checkout is a turnoff."

WHAT THINGS DO YOU MOST LIKE ABOUT A SHOPPING EXPERIENCE?

Number five: Fast checkout   4.5%

Your customer wants fast checkout. In our surveys, checkout speed was mentioned by 1 of every 20 consumers.

Number four: Merchandise organized and easy to find   8.8%

One in every 11 survey respondents mentioned that the ability to quickly and easily locate merchandise was important.

Number three: Low prices and product information   18.3%

Strangely, low prices went hand-in-hand with the desire for product information in the nature of hanging tags or shelf talkers that would assist the consumer with the purchase decision. Notice that price, while important, was not as important with everyone and should by no means be considered a deal breaker in even a majority of cases.

Number two: Courteous/friendly/caring staff   27%

More than one in four consumers used the specific term courteous or friendly or caring. This is a soft skill, one that you hire instead of train for. Customers were saying hire someone who likes me and who I will like as well. They weren't looking for rocket scientists, just nice people who enjoy their work, and who at least appear to like their customers.

Number one: Knowledgeable, helpful salespeople   41.4%

Every second or third customer who walked through your doors was looking for a salesperson who knew his or her stuff and willingly shared it. But wait! There's more!

A close look at the verbatim responses revealed that customers wanted knowledgeable assistance, on their terms. Over and over again, customers told us they hated pushy salespeople. Time and time again, customers told us that when they didn't want help to please leave them alone. On the other hand, they wanted sales staff to be easy to find, but only when they were wanted. They were saying, "Make yourself scarce but don't go too far!"

Here's a look at the list in a more familiar order:

Knowledgeable/Helpful salespeople	41.4%
Courteous/Friendly/Caring staff	27.0%
Low prices and product information	18.3%
Merchandise organized and easy to find	8.8%
Fast checkout	4.5%
	100.0%

Now that we know what customers want, two questions immediately come to mind: Who is doing a good job? and How do they do it?

The easiest thing to do would be to rate the top retailers, figure out which is number one, and say, "Do what they do." Easy, but wrong. Alliance Data Systems ranked the top-100 specialty stores in the August 2004 issue of *Stores* magazine. You could copy the top dog, but if you don't sell home electronics, there isn't much in imitating number-one-ranked Best Buy. Numbers two and three would have you selling youthful fashion or office supplies, à la Gap and Staples.

Even the best of the best isn't number one in each of the five categories revealed by our surveys. So, we'll check out who is best by category and find out how they managed to get that way.

THE DEFINITION OF *IS*

This first dimension of knowledgeable/helpful salespeople opens a small can of worms. Knowledgeable at Circuit City is entirely different from knowledgeable at Wal-Mart. At Circuit City, you might ask about gigabytes or megapixels, while at Wal-Mart, a fastball might be as difficult as "Where are the shorts?"

As a famous American once said, "It depends on what the definition of *is* is." However you define it, knowledgeable/helpful staff is the number one most important thing to a whopping 41.4 percent of consumers.

Knowledgeable and helpful are both concepts defined solely by the customer. At Home Depot, a salesperson might need the knowledge and experience of a master plumber and be required to cough it up at a far lower hourly rate. Because knowledgeable and helpful are product-dependent, we won't name the best all-around; instead, we'll look at a few categories where the consumer has spoken.

Price also seems to matter depending on the category of product. Overall, 18.3 percent of our sample group primarily base their shopping decision on price/promotion. So, just for fun, we'll do double duty in our analysis and look at knowledgeable/helpful simultaneous with price/promotion and see how these and other dimensions might work together in shaping our decision about where we shop and buy.

MEN'S CLOTHING

Figure 8.1 indicates that when asked where they shopped most for men's clothing, 21.4 percent of our sample group (men and women 18 years or older) indicated Wal-Mart. But only 11.5 percent of the entire sample thought that Wal-Mart was the place to find knowledgeable/helpful associates in the men's department. If we consider average as being an index of 100, Wal-Mart performs at about half of average with an index of only 54.

There must be another reason why 21.4 percent of consumers shop most often for men's clothes at Wal-Mart. Hmm, I wonder what that could be. Do I see a smiley face?

Look further down at Dillard's with an index of 366, indicating that Dillard's most frequent customers for men's clothing grade the staff in the men's department as knowledgeable and helpful at a rate in excess of three times average. But Dillard's only captures 1.6 percent of shoppers for men's clothing. You might infer that marketwide, knowledgeable and helpful aren't going to draw a crowd in this category.

A quick glance at the far right column shows that Wal-Mart, Kmart, Old Navy, Target, and Kohl's are duking it out on price. Look way to the bottom and you'll see that the discount stores as a group (148) are beat by membership warehouses (151) and the Internet (149).

The reason all of the categories, except "other," have indexes greater than 100 is a large number of consumers selected "no preference" as their store shopped most for men's clothing. Looking at the top line of this chart, notice that of 9,232 respondents, only 540 choose knowledgeable/helpful staff as most important, while 5,835 were in the background chanting "stack 'em deep and sell 'em cheap." This is probably a reflection on men and those who buy for them. My guess is these consumers think there is so little difference in men's clothing that the where and what of the decision are not that important.

FIGURE 8.1 *Men's Clothing*

Knowledgeable sales-people vs. price	ALL, 18+	Men's, Knowledge	Index	Men's, Price	Index
Count	9,232	540		5,835	
Men's Clothing (Shop at Most Often)					
Wal-Mart	21.4%	11.5%	54	31.7%	149
JCPenney	8.4%	15.0%	177	10.7%	127
Kohl's	4.9%	4.0%	82	6.8%	140
Sears	4.4%	5.6%	128	5.1%	117
Target	3.1%	1.7%	54	4.5%	145
Kmart	2.7%	1.6%	60	4.0%	148
Old Navy	2.3%	1.4%	62	3.4%	147
Dillard's	1.6%	6.0%	366	1.7%	101
Mervyns	1.4%	2.3%	164	1.8%	129
Gap	1.1%	1.9%	185	1.2%	110
Macy's	1.0%	2.5%	249	1.2%	115
Ross	0.7%	0.6%	89	1.0%	154
Marshalls	0.6%	0.5%	83	0.9%	153
Meijer	0.6%	1.4%	241	0.8%	136
Other	21.2%	40.7%	192	22.2%	105
No preference	24.7%	3.3%	13	3.1%	12
Total	100.0%	100.0%		100.0%	
Men's Clothing (Shop at Most Often)					
Department store	27.3%	47.9%	175	33.2%	121
Discount store	30.4%	18.2%	60	44.9%	148
Specialty—Apparel	9.1%	18.6%	204	9.4%	103
Membership warehouse	0.7%	0.0%	0	1.1%	151
Catalog	0.9%	1.0%	111	0.9%	105
Internet	0.2%	0.0%	0	0.3%	149
Other	6.7%	11.1%	167	7.2%	108
No preference	24.7%	3.3%	13	3.1%	12
Total	100.0%	100.0%		100.0%	
What are the reasons you buy your men's clothing there? (Check all that apply.)					
Price	64.2%	76.8%	120	100.0%	156
Selection	53.2%	92.9%	175	69.6%	131
Location	38.2%	59.5%	156	53.0%	139
Quality	39.8%	91.3%	229	50.1%	126
Service	13.6%	69.9%	512	18.0%	132
Fashion ideas	6.4%	26.2%	407	6.9%	107

(continued)

FIGURE 8.1 *Men's Clothing (Continued)*

Knowledgeable sales-people vs. price	ALL, 18+	Men's, Knowledge	Index	Men's, Price	Index
Newest styles	8.4%	36.4%	431	10.1%	119
Newest fabrics	3.5%	23.0%	662	4.2%	120
Knowledgeable salespeople	6.6%	100.0%	1525	7.8%	120
Store appearance	9.6%	50.1%	524	11.8%	124
Store layout	9.9%	41.6%	422	13.2%	134
Other	6.1%	5.4%	88	3.7%	61

The sum of the percent totals may be greater than 100 percent because the respondents can select more than one answer.
Source: BIGresearch, Consumer Intentions and Actions, July 2004.

HOME IMPROVEMENT

Now let's check out the winners in the home improvement category. (See Figure 8.2.) Home Depot, Lowe's, and Ace Hardware all had indexes well over 100. Ace Hardware weighed in with a stunning 184, beating both Home Depot and Lowe's in knowledgeable/helpful employees. Ace Hardware really is the place with the helpful hardware man. Too bad the customer saw them as being a bit pricey with an index for price of only 77. Notice, we did not say that Ace Hardware was more expensive, only that the consumer thought it was.

Now watch this: In terms of knowledgeable/friendly staff, Home Depot beat Lowe's (134 vs. 119). But both shared the same score for price (117). All things being equal, Home Depot had the advantage in markets where the two stores were side-by-side or nearly so.

But all things aren't equal. People value other things than knowledgeable/helpful staff. They also tell us that new ideas and products, installation service, even store appearance are all factors in where they choose to shop. Men apparently pay more attention to their power tools than their power suits. Of 8,701 respondents, 2,413 said knowledgeable/helpful salespeople count more than price (5,990).

WOMEN'S CLOTHING

Women's clothing shoppers appeared to prefer to have their personal style pretty much dialed in by the time they reached 18. These shoppers were interested in bargains. They have been trained to sniff for bargains, which must be the female version of hunting and gathering.

FIGURE 8.2 *Home Improvement/Hardware*

Knowledgeable salespeople vs. price	ALL, 18+	Home Improvement, Knowledge	Index	Home Improvement, Price	Index
Count	8,701	2,413		5,990	
Home Improvement/Hardware (Shop at Most Often)					
Home Depot	35.6%	47.8%	134	41.7%	117
Lowe's	22.7%	27.0%	119	26.6%	117
Wal-Mart	5.8%	1.4%	24	8.4%	145
Menards	4.6%	4.9%	106	5.9%	128
Ace Hardware	2.6%	4.8%	184	2.0%	77
Sears	1.1%	1.1%	106	1.2%	114
True Value	0.7%	0.8%	118	0.5%	75
Other	7.3%	10.5%	144	7.5%	104
No preference	19.7%	1.8%	9	6.0%	31
Total	100.0%	100.0%		100.0%	
Home Improvement/Hardware (Shop at Most Often)					
Department store	1.1%	1.1%	102	1.2%	113
Discount store	6.9%	2.3%	33	9.7%	141
Specialty—Hardlines	0.1%	0.0%	0	0.1%	152
Membership warehouse	0.0%	0.0%	0	0.1%	152
Home improvement store	67.0%	86.5%	129	77.8%	116
Catalog	0.0%	0.0%	0	0.0%	0
Internet	0.0%	0.0%	0	0.0%	152
Other	5.2%	8.3%	158	5.0%	96
No preference	19.7%	1.8%	9	6.0%	31
Total	100.0%	100.0%		100.0%	
What are the reasons you buy your home improvement/hardware there? (Check all that apply.)					
Price	65.6%	81.7%	124	100.0%	152
Selection	62.8%	88.0%	140	79.5%	127
Location	57.2%	72.2%	126	67.6%	118
Quality	44.1%	75.4%	171	57.9%	131
Service	32.7%	70.3%	215	42.3%	129
Financing options	3.9%	8.5%	221	5.2%	134
Store appearance	10.9%	27.2%	249	14.4%	132
Store layout	16.3%	36.9%	227	21.0%	129
Home improvement ideas/tips	20.6%	47.8%	232	26.6%	129

(continued)

FIGURE 8.2 *Home Improvement/Hardware (Continued)*

Knowledgeable salespeople vs. price	ALL, 18+	Home Improvement, Knowledge	Index	Home Improvement, Price	Index
Newest styles/products	10.8%	28.4%	262	14.5%	134
Installation services	7.3%	21.2%	289	9.4%	128
Knowledgeable salespeople	25.9%	100.0%	386	32.2%	124
Other	3.2%	2.8%	86	1.9%	59

The sum of the percent totals may be greater than 100 percent because the respondents can select more than one answer.
Source: BIGresearch, Consumer Intentions and Actions, June 2004.

In our sample of 7,498, only 574 selected their favorite shopping destination based primarily on knowledgeable/helpful staff. The rest, 5,373, were heading for the clearance racks. (See Figure 8.3 on page 149.)

More shoppers of women's clothing shopped mostly at Wal-Mart than any other store. Wal-Mart beat JCPenney by a factor of three! But why did they choose Wally World? Price! (Index of 158)

Look down the chart at Lane Bryant, where knowledgeable/helpful might also be defined as nonjudgmental, with an index of 182. Do Lane Bryant shoppers go for the prices with a price index of only 98? Not even. Lane Bryant shoppers know that for selection in larger sizes, nobody beats Lane Bryant.

LINENS/BEDDING/DRAPERIES

In the category of linens/bedding/draperies, price was even more important than the quality of the staff. (See Figure 8.4 on page 151.) Wal-Mart, again, was the big dog, capturing first choice of 27.1 percent of U.S. consumers. While only 17.6 percent thought Wal-Mart was a great place to encounter a knowledgeable/helpful staff (index of 65), it was a great place to hear the sound of another price going down (index of 139).

Linens 'n Things is where to go when you need an expert eye. Why? Because with an index of 256, of the majors they were clearly the most knowledgeable in the business.

FIGURE 8.3 *Women's Clothing*

Knowledgeable salespeople vs. price	ALL, 18+	Women's, Knowledge	Index	Women's, Price	Index
Count	7,498	574		5,373	
Women's Clothing (Shop at Most Often)					
Wal-Mart	18.9%	16.3%	86	29.8%	158
JCPenney	6.2%	7.8%	127	8.1%	132
Kohl's	5.0%	3.6%	73	7.4%	150
Target	2.7%	2.9%	108	4.2%	157
Sears	2.3%	3.9%	169	2.8%	123
Kmart	2.2%	1.4%	63	3.3%	152
Lane Bryant	1.9%	3.5%	182	1.9%	98
Old Navy	1.9%	1.2%	65	2.8%	150
Fashion Bug	1.6%	2.8%	170	2.3%	140
Dillard's	1.4%	3.3%	230	1.3%	87
Macy's	1.3%	4.0%	319	1.7%	130
Ross	1.2%	0.7%	55	2.0%	163
T.J. Maxx	0.9%	0.4%	42	1.5%	163
Mervyns	0.9%	0.4%	49	1.1%	130
Bealls	0.6%	1.1%	180	0.9%	145
Blair	0.6%	0.0%	0	0.9%	157
Marshalls	0.6%	0.4%	71	0.8%	150
Other	22.2%	43.6%	197	25.5%	115
No preference	27.8%	2.7%	10	1.8%	7
Total	100.0%	100.0%		100.0%	
Women's Clothing (Shop at Most Often)					
Department store	24.2%	37.7%	156	31.4%	130
Discount store	27.2%	22.4%	82	42.6%	157
Specialty—Apparel	12.9%	25.7%	198	14.8%	114
Membership warehouse	0.1%	0.0%	0	0.2%	151
Catalog	1.2%	0.6%	48	1.6%	132
Internet	0.4%	0.0%	0	0.6%	149
Other	6.2%	11.0%	177	7.1%	114
No preference	27.8%	2.7%	10	1.8%	7
Total	100.0%	100.0%		100.0%	
What are the reasons you buy your women's clothing there? (Check all that apply.)					
Price	61.4%	76.5%	124	100.0%	163
Selection	53.1%	88.1%	166	74.0%	139
Location	39.3%	67.6%	172	56.7%	144

(continued)

FIGURE 8.3 *Women's Clothing (Continued)*

Knowledgeable salespeople vs. price	ALL, 18+	Women's, Knowledge	Index	Women's, Price	Index
Quality	39.6%	85.1%	215	53.5%	135
Service	17.3%	76.9%	444	24.2%	140
Fashion ideas	11.7%	44.2%	378	15.3%	130
Newest styles	13.0%	47.1%	362	17.4%	134
Newest fabrics	5.0%	30.1%	608	6.8%	138
Knowledgeable salespeople	7.8%	100.0%	1278	9.7%	124
Other	5.5%	4.4%	80	4.0%	73

The sum of the percent totals may be greater than 100 percent because the respondents can select more than one answer.
Source: BIGresearch, Consumer Intentions and Actions, May 2004.

CONSUMER ELECTRONICS

Electronics, as you might expect, requires a bit more of the sales staff. Of our 8,725 panelists, just over 20 percent (1,749) primarily based their choice on the availability of knowledgeable/helpful staff. (See Figure 8.5 on page 152.)

In this category, in spite of a relatively small sample, Radio Shack got the nod as the home of knowledgeable/helpful staff (index of 247, two-and-a-half times the average). Too bad the market saw them as a tad on the pricey side (index of 63).

Circuit City was the best of the big players, although Best Buy probably had a better buy.

COURTEOUS EMPLOYEES

Notice that this dimension seems similar to knowledgeable/helpful. It's not. The actual description is "courteous/friendly/caring staff." Where knowledgeable/helpful could be interpreted as "know their product and are willing to share that knowledge," courteous/friendly/caring has more to do with likability, or, in short, nice people.

Of our sample group, 27 percent said that nice people were the number one factor in shaping their feelings about a retailer. (See Figure 8.6 on page 154.)

Nordstrom customers say Nordstrom salespeople are likely to be courteous/friendly/caring at a rate of more than three times average.

FIGURE 8.4 *Linens/Bedding/Draperies*

Knowledgeable sales-people vs. price	ALL, 18+	Linens, Knowledge	Index	Linens, Price	Index
Count	7,774	472		5,734	
Linens/Bedding/Draperies (Shop at Most Often)					
Wal-Mart	27.1%	17.6%	65	37.7%	139
JCPenney	8.5%	22.5%	264	9.1%	107
Bed Bath & Beyond	6.1%	13.6%	224	5.9%	96
Target	5.6%	1.8%	33	7.7%	137
Sears	4.6%	7.1%	155	4.5%	99
Kmart	3.9%	2.3%	59	5.1%	131
Linens 'n Things	3.8%	9.7%	256	3.8%	100
Kohl's	1.9%	1.3%	71	2.2%	120
Mervyns	0.6%	0.8%	138	0.7%	131
Other	15.3%	18.9%	123	18.0%	117
No preference	22.6%	4.3%	19	5.2%	23
Total	100.0%	100.0%		100.0%	
Linens/Bedding/Draperies (Shop at Most Often)					
Department store	18.7%	38.3%	205	19.6%	105
Discount store	39.7%	22.0%	55	54.3%	137
Specialty—Apparel	0.3%	0.1%	25	0.4%	127
Membership warehouse	0.5%	0.0%	0	0.7%	142
Catalog	0.7%	0.5%	74	0.8%	106
Internet	0.5%	0.2%	33	0.6%	136
Other	17.0%	31.6%	201	18.1%	109
No preference	22.6%	4.3%	19	5.2%	23
Total	100.0%	100.0%		100.0%	
What are the reasons you buy your linens/bedding/draperies there? (Check all that apply.)					
Price	69.2%	84.5%	122	100.0%	144
Selection	48.9%	88.0%	180	59.3%	121
Location	36.0%	58.9%	163	45.2%	126
Quality	37.7%	85.3%	226	44.6%	118
Service	12.5%	62.4%	499	15.6%	125
Fashion ideas	6.0%	33.7%	556	7.4%	123
Newest styles	6.2%	34.1%	546	7.5%	120
Newest fabrics	4.3%	31.4%	732	5.4%	126
Knowledgeable salespeople	6.0%	100.0%	1659	7.4%	122
Other	3.4%	2.2%	64	2.0%	59

The sum of the percent totals may be greater than 100 percent because the respondents can select more than one answer.
Source: BIGresearch, Consumer Intentions and Actions, April 2004.

FIGURE 8.5 *Consumer Electronics*

Knowledgeable sales-people vs. price	ALL, 18+	Electronics, Knowledge	Index	Electronics, Price	Index
Count	8,725	1,749		6,832	
Electronics (TVs, DVDs, etc.) (Shop at Most Often)					
Best Buy	27.9%	43.0%	154	32.6%	117
Wal-Mart	22.1%	8.6%	39	27.5%	124
Circuit City	8.8%	16.4%	186	9.5%	108
Sears	5.0%	5.6%	113	4.9%	100
Target	1.9%	1.2%	64	2.3%	121
Sam's Club	1.2%	0.7%	55	1.6%	129
Radio Shack	1.2%	3.0%	247	0.8%	63
Fry's	1.0%	1.4%	137	1.3%	122
Costco	1.0%	0.4%	37	1.3%	127
Kmart	1.0%	0.6%	60	1.1%	120
Other	11.4%	16.6%	146	12.6%	111
No preference	17.4%	2.6%	15	4.4%	25
Total	100.0%	100.0%		100.0%	
Electronics (TVs, DVDs, etc.) (Shop at Most Often)					
Department store	5.1%	5.7%	113	5.1%	100
Discount store	25.4%	10.5%	41	31.4%	123
Specialty—Hardlines	41.7%	68.9%	165	47.4%	114
Membership warehouse	2.6%	1.3%	50	3.3%	128
Home improvement store	0.2%	0.2%	148	0.2%	122
Catalog	0.0%	0.0%	0	0.0%	110
Internet	1.3%	0.3%	21	1.5%	119
Other	6.3%	10.5%	166	6.7%	106
No preference	17.4%	2.6%	15	4.4%	25
Total	100.0%	100.0%		100.0%	
What are the reasons you buy your electronics there? (Check all that apply.)					
Price	77.4%	90.2%	117	100.0%	129
Selection	59.8%	89.7%	150	71.0%	119
Location	46.5%	60.2%	130	54.2%	117
Quality	40.5%	76.3%	188	48.2%	119
Service	30.5%	71.4%	234	35.8%	117
Good financing options	7.7%	20.4%	265	9.1%	118
Knowledgeable salespeople	20.5%	100.0%	488	23.9%	117

FIGURE 8.5 *Consumer Electronics (Continued)*

Knowledgeable sales-people vs. price	ALL, 18+	Electronics, Knowledge	Index	Electronics, Price	Index
Have installation service for car, truck, and SUV	2.6%	8.8%	337	3.3%	126
Have latest high-tech products	15.4%	40.1%	260	18.1%	118
Other	3.5%	2.3%	66	2.3%	65

The sum of the percent totals may be greater than 100 percent because the respondents can select more than one answer.
Source: BIGresearch, Consumer Intentions and Actions, March 2004.

That's no surprise. They work in a pleasant environment for a company known worldwide for flawless customer service. And, this is just a guess, my bet is that salespeople who are really great at customer service are attracted to a company where great service is celebrated.

But Wal-Mart? Let's see, you get to wait on a mass of humanity who clearly did not come for the service, the environment is anything but elegant, and the sheer volume of inventory, people, noise, and screeching PAs is, at idle, a dull roar. But hey, we just did the survey; the customers delivered their opinions, and we certainly didn't mess with the numbers.

Wal-Mart, as you can see, was seen as a place for finding courteous/friendly/caring staff at a rate almost double the ordinary retailer (179).

Among the majors, there were only a few other standouts and a whole pack of disappointments. At Walgreens, we had a problem (17).

Home Depot and Lowe's, both cited by our panel for knowledgeable employees, could use a trip to charm school. Neither operator came close to batting the league average (37 and 48, respectively).

ORGANIZED MERCHANDISE

The champion of organized, easy-to-find merchandise is Wal-Mart (227). Why? How about several thousand look-alike stores? If you can find car polish at the Wal-Mart in Boise, chances are you can head straight for the auto department at the Wal-Mart in Kerrville, Texas.

Shoppers who make well-organized merchandise their primary reason for selecting a retailer accounted for 8.8 percent of our survey population. (See Figure 8.7 on page 155.) We think that organized and easy-to-find translates as easy in, easy out. Chili's wants your business when they say get in, get out, get on with your life. They understand that many of us want the product without the hassle.

FIGURE 8.6 *Courteous Employees*

Retailer	Index
Nordstrom	318
Wal-Mart	179
Meijer	148
Safeway	130
Target	115
Kroger	88
Kohl's	84
Albertsons	81
Sam's Club	70
Costco	69
Lowe's	48
Publix	46
Kmart	44
Best Buy	39
Home Depot	37
JCPenney	36
Sears	25
Walgreens	17

Source: BIGresearch.

We imagine that the group that reported organized and easy-to-find were conflicted, that they couldn't also claim fast checkout as being important in their decision-making process.

It's odd to think that Sam's Club (58) got such low marks being from the same family as Wal-Mart. It wasn't even as good as Kmart (66), but probably for two very different reasons. At Sam's the merchandise is constantly changing, while at Kmart financial difficulties have made for reported out-of-stock situations.

Easy-to-find merchandise is important, but not as important as encountering a pleasant, helpful display once you find the merchandise. Merchandising could be defined as "displaying merchandise in such a way that shoppers are motivated to buy." Organized and easy-to-find isn't nearly the same as effectively merchandized. And who does a great job of merchandising? Customers said it's Nordstrom. But the sample is small, and Nordstrom is hardly the store for everyman. (See Figure 8.8 on page 156.)

FIGURE 8.7 *Merchandise Is Easy to Find*

Retailer	Index
Wal-Mart	227
Meijer	193
Target	184
Safeway	106
Kroger	98
Costco	75
Albertsons	75
Kohl's	70
Kmart	66
Sam's Club	58
Publix	43
Best Buy	26
JCPenney	23
Sears	21
Lowe's	20
Home Depot	14

Source: BIGresearch.

Of the majors, Best Buy was the big dog of the specialty stores (454), while Target led the discount department stores (381). Dollar Stores (7), Big Lots (8), Dollar General (13), and Family Dollar (14) might get away with calling disheveled merchandising as part of their appeal, but Kmart (12) and Ross (14)? Certainly, when we see who is swimming at the bottom of the barrel, Kmart can least afford to be there. If the customer is any indication, Kmart isn't sinking; they have already sunk.

FAST CHECKOUT

Our grandson, Big Guy, loves a good story. He and the Princess will often say, "Pops! Let's go to the storytelling room (den) and you can tell us a story." The Princess will ask for a story about a little girl with big blue eyes, but the Big Guy, no doubt bound for the corporate world, will ask for "something really scary, Pops. No happiness."

If there is one place where customers are least likely to expect happiness, it must be the checkout line. (See Figure 8.9 on page 157.) The bad news is that we don't expect much from the checkout experience. It has been so bad for so long that consumer expectations have lowered the bar so far, retailers no longer have to jump over it. They can step

FIGURE 8.8   *Which retailer is best and which is worst at merchandising the products it sells? (For instance, are the products close together, the aisles overflowing, prices clear, etc.?)*

Rank	Retailer	Scorecard
1	Nordstrom	849
2	Best Buy	454
3	Target	381
4	Costco	209
5	Meijer	186
6	Kohl's	165
7	Lowe's	158
8	Wal-Mart	141
9	Sam's Club	135
10	Sears	122
	Walgreens	99
	JCPenney	88
	Home Depot	66
6	Ross	14
5	Family Dollar	14
4	Dollar General	13
3	Kmart	12
2	Big Lots	8
1	Dollar Store	7

Source: BIGresearch, July 2004 (n = 9,232).

over it simply by opening another register. They can leap over it by removing chewing gum, personal conversations, and cell phones. A touch of eye contact will send consumers to retail heaven.

The good news is that today's customer no longer expects much from the checkout experience. Only 4.5 percent any longer have a bug about checkout. The rest have simply given up.

CONTAIN YOURSELF

No doubt there are plenty of small retailers that look at the giants and think "if only . . ." But every large retailer started out . . . well, you get the picture. Have you ever wondered what Sam Walton thought about while he tried to grow his little store into a retail giant?

FIGURE 8.9 *Fast Checkout Lines*

Retailer	Index
Target	199
Meijer	189
Wal-Mart	154
Kroger	130
Safeway	124
Albertsons	92
Winn Dixie	91
Kohl's	66
Sam's Club	61
Kmart	52
Publix	50
Lowe's	23
Home Depot	17
Sears	15

When you read the stories of this country's retail pioneers, there is always a set of underlying values that are credited for the success of what started as merely a dream. Don't you wonder if maybe the values were added later in the game, that it was something cooked up by the training or marketing departments?

For a look at how the best of the best become the biggest of the best, let's look at a company that was founded in recent history, where the values were there at the start and not added as an historic afterthought. This company didn't register on our list of the best of the best—too small, too regional, but not about to be missed by this writer. *Fortune* magazine recognized them as one of the top-five best companies to work for, and we recognize them as eminently qualified to serve as an example of two-of-five retailing virtues: knowledgeable/helpful employees and friendly/caring employees. Isn't it nice to discover that excelling in one area does not exclude you from the other?

Who is this gifted retailer? It's a company with both heart and soul—The Container Store, the used-to-be-Dallas-only chain specializing in "things in which to keep your stuff." Can you imagine what the bankers thought about that business plan?

Who would have predicted that for the last five years, the little group that could, would be recognized by *Fortune* as one of America's best places to work? Today The Container Store is a model of a workforce that is both knowledgeable and caring. It has a lock on the top two elements for creating happy customers. (As a customer, I think it scores at the top of the pack in all five!)

THE VALUABLE VALUES

The Container Store folks refer to them as the Foundation Principles.™ They are so serious about this, that the term is trademarked! So I'm going to paraphrase; they are better retailers, but I'm a better writer! Here they are, a road map to success if you are brave enough to follow it.

Do Unto Others

The Container Store takes the long route when it says, "Fill the other guy's basket to the brim. Making money then becomes an easy proposition." The idea is to avoid the dog-eat-dog world of traditional retailing, where retailers beat up the suppliers and then cut prices so low that service goes straight out the window. The Container Store pays vendors on time on the theory that well-treated vendors will be loyal and more likely to bring new ideas and products to the folks who treat them best.

Sell the Solution

The Container Store calls it "man in the desert." It's a miniparable that goes something like this: If you stumbled upon a man lost in the desert, you might offer him water, which is what the traditional retailer might be expected to do. But, speculates The Container Store corporate culture, maybe he needs something in addition to water. He may need food, fresh clothing, or a lift to the nearest town. This guy, says The Container Store people, needs a complete solution.

Okay, so it's simple upselling, but if it's so easy, how come the most creative thing most retail clerks say is, "May I help you?" The Container Store associates are trained to ask questions and then listen when the customers talk.

Fewer, Better People

In The Container Store culture, there exists a curious equation that looks something like this: One average person equals three lousy people. One good person equals three average people, and one great person equals three good people. The math continues: In terms of business productivity, a great person is three times as productive as the ordinary person. So the logic goes, if you hire great people, who are three times as productive, you can pay them twice as much, and still have yourself a bargain.

Does it work? The shareholders say it does, a thought that is seconded by The Container Store customers. Personally, I think The Container Store math is a bit off. Benefits for The Container Store employees are remarkable in the truest sense of the word. Full-time employees can expect world-class health care, including eight weeks paid maternity leave, two weeks if you're the papa. Once hired, you can expect ongoing store discounts of 40 percent plus surprise employee purchase programs that come when The Container Store partners with suppliers to come up with special, employee-only deals.

At The Container Store, vacation time is generous and quickly turns into paid sabbaticals. At corporate, you can join a yoga class for free or just sit at your desk to wait for the regular visits by a masseuse for a chair massage. But wait! There's more! A lot more. We've said enough, however, and besides, what would happen if one of your employees happened to see the complete list?

This is how you build a staff that is courteous/friendly/caring. Even if you have managed to hire naturally caring individuals, their ability to exercise that natural ability has a lot to do with how they are treated. When you love the staff, watch them love the customer.

Train, Train, Train

This is where the knowledgeable/helpful salespeople come in. The Container Store likes to quote, "Intuition does not come to an unprepared mind. You need to train before it happens." And train they do. First year, full-time employees receive more than 241 hours of training. Compare that to what you are familiar with (seven hours is industry standard), and you'll see there is no comparison.

Simultaneous Selection, Service, and Price

The Container Store values leave no space for what everyone in business knows to be irrefutable truth: selection, service, price—pick any two. The Container Store says, no way! You can have it all, and The Container Store has set its sights on consistently delivering all three.

Keep 'Em Pumped

The Container Store moves motivation (and training) from the back room onto the sales floor, where customers can sense and share the "air of excitement." If these ideas appeared in a management seminar, it would be fair, maybe even wise, to be skeptical. But they didn't. They're playing daily in broad daylight in little stores that sell containers for your stuff!

WHOSE MA?

Every business is a mom-and-pop operation. No matter how big the company or the store, somebody's ma or pa is in charge. It's not important to run the best store in the world, just the best in your market. You don't have to beat Wal-Mart or be better than every Lowe's; you just have to be better than the store down the street. As we have seen, the most important elements of the retail experience are controlled at store level.

All you have to do is *listen* when customers talk.

For more information, visit http://www.whencustomerstalk.com.

9

ON THE HORIZON

In 1994, *Fortune* named the Won-
derbra as one of its products of the year. No doubt, the magazine is run
by men. Still, the selection does stand out (pardon the pun) as a sign of
the times. Even *Fortune* was amused by the choice and covered their
tracks saying, ". . . if naming a brassiere one of *Fortune*'s Products of the
Year has a message, it is that new approaches, new technology . . . new
ideas . . . can turn a humbling commodity into a hot one."

TECHNOLOGY

Shoppers who use the new technology tend to be younger by three
to six years than the average shopper, higher-than-average earners, and
more likely to have a college degree. They also are more likely to have
children under 18 living in their homes. (That explains it! The kids are
showing them how to use the technology!)

They may also be older and less urban than you might expect. Several years ago, I was invited to speak to the folks at Viking-White, the
makers of sophisticated, Internet-connected sewing machines. I expected an audience of genteel ladies, many from small towns in the
heartland, wearing denim vests with embroidered flowers. I was right
on the money. Well, sort of.

What surprised me was how tech-savvy this group was. They were so well connected with one another via the Internet that the annual corporate road show to unveil the newest models was canceled mid-schedule. Why? The ladies—and they were mostly ladies—in the early cities of the road show couldn't wait to jump on the grapevine and tell the folks later in the schedule. By the time corporate had made their second or third stop, the surprise was gone.

Technology will become an increasingly important part of the shopping experience. Some of the new technology will be the predictable evolution of existing technology, but some of it will be simply incredible!

Disruptive Technology

Clayton Christensen (*Innovator's Dilemma*, Harvard Business School Press, 1997) coined the term *disruptive technology*. We expanded the original definition, which focused on technology, to include process as well and called it Disruptive Thinking (DT). DT is any process or technology that alters the economic fundamentals of a market or market segment.

There are dozens of technologies that deserve mention, but we'll pick only one: Voice recognition and embedded intelligence are about to change the way products and people interact. Voice recognition technology is estimated to grow by 97 percent in 2004. Currently, it is 95 percent accurate, and by 2013, dictation is expected to equal human accuracy. "The appliances and machines around us will soon remember us individually and anticipate our needs." (Rogers and Pepper, *Enterprise One to One*, Currency, 1997)

If my house remembers that I like the room cooler at night with my programmable thermostat, why can't you (the retailer) remember I wear a 42 long sport coat, that my airplane uses 20-50 XC oil, or that I am on a low-carb diet except for chocolate cake?

What makes DT so disruptive is it usually requires a substantial investment in technology. But established companies with significant investment in infrastructure insist on trying to wring more out of existing tech and get killed when the market suddenly turns. Discounters finally get to department stores. Discount airlines get to the other airlines. Disk drive manufacturers lose out to chips.

Not all DT is negative. Even the new Transportation Safety Administration (TSA) has its positive attributes, such as the touch screen terminals that allow you to bypass the line and quickly retrieve your boarding pass.

Scan me! Could you have predicted this one? Researchers at MIT have invented a handheld device that will allow consumers to scan the bar code on a product and get instant feedback about the social responsibility of the manufacturer. Set up to click like a Geiger counter, the worse the company's record on pollution, use of poorly compensated third world labor, and other social issues, the louder and faster it will click.

This is all very interesting, but not likely to be as popular as the device in the wings at Microsoft. A research sociologist at Microsoft figured that a handheld bar code scanner could be employed to trigger a wireless Internet search to discover ingredients that might trigger an allergy or upset a special diet. Techno-shoppers could set the device to search based on any area of interest, from corporate policies toward women to support of various social and political groups.

The big question that remains is, In the end, just how important will these issues be compared to the traditional price-value ratio?

Not all DT is positive. When was the last time you paid the exorbitant rates for using a hotel telephone? If you are a hotelier, no doubt you fail to see the widespread use of cell phones as a positive influence on the bottom line. Hotels have gone from "we gotcha" to Marriott's most recent offer of unlimited Internet access and unlimited long distance calls for $9.95!

Not all DT is recognized for what it is. Disruptive thinking, rarely seen from a distance, gives it its disruptive power. In 1976, when Lamar Muse and Herb Kelleher drew up the plans for Southwest Airlines on a cocktail napkin, who would have a guessed they were planting the seeds of an idea that would, eventually, totally disrupt the economics of commercial aviation? Flying a single aircraft type point-to-point is disruptive thinking at its best.

Looking at that napkin, who would have thought: United Airlines and Delta Airlines would both start discount look-alikes? Who would have figured there would be a JetBlue? And who would have imagined that Southwest Airlines and JetBlue would be the most profitable, if not the only profitable, airlines in 2003?

After sharing the definition of DT with a friend, he casually mentioned that his 17-year-old daughter had not purchased a music CD in years, that she and her friends ripped and burned direct from the Internet. Coincidentally, while driving through San Antonio and later in the week through Los Angeles, we happened across the same going-out-of-business sign for Wherehouse Music stores, a national chain. Who would have thought that a 17-year-old looking for nothing more than her favorite music could close a national business?

And then Starbucks turns right around and uses the same technology that closed one national chain to open another called Hear Music Coffeehouse!

Here's a rhetorical question: What well-intentioned bureaucrat, ill-intentioned terrorist, or brilliant scientist with no intentions other than discovery could bring your business to an end?

WHAT IS NOT LIKELY TO CHANGE

Human nature is not likely to change. People do business with people, but the context in which we express our nature is subject to dramatic change: Purchase decisions will continue to be based on emotions, and finding employees willing to play to those emotions will continue to be our biggest problem.

Today there is technology for ensuring good, maybe even great, hires, but you have to use it. And there are interviewing techniques that will have dishonest employees admitting their lack of integrity before you find out the hard way. When are you going to start using profiling technology for hiring and promotion decisions?

WHAT IF . . .

In the NASA aerospace commission report, the authors pose an attractive proposition: What if, just what if, commercial airlines ran on time . . . always? That's DT! And what if technology could make the flying (or landing) environment equally attractive without regard to size of the airport? And what if the airlines were to make flying attractive again by serving even small cities economically and conveniently? What would that do to your business?

What if technology puts a GPS-based precision approach on any and every runway? The value of airport real estate suddenly changes. Small town airports with reasonably long runways become attractive for fuel stops, while at the same time the threat of terrorism in major cities makes those same secondary markets more attractive for meetings, tourism, and even corporate headquarters. If you operate in small towns already, how would that change your planning? And what if you don't operate in small towns? Would easy access make a difference to you or your customers? And that's without Bill Aycock and his AirFlite idea to bring low-cost, on-demand air taxi service to Americans everywhere!

And what if the airlines got serious about courting corporate aviation? If an airline were to call me for consulting, I would have to tell them that corporate travelers need to be wooed instead of robbed.

Speaking of transportation, here's a surprise: The cost of a new automobile in real dollars is going down, not up, and that's not even considering the improvements brought by new technology. Each year, automakers are building better cars and trucks for less than the previous year. It's happening to products in every category, so we ask, "If next year's model will be better and less expensive, what is my motivation for buying this year?"

What if suddenly your biggest competitor doubled in size? What if they went out of business? What if we began to focus on where our customers were going? Who has ever figured out how to make money based on knowing the customer's next shopping destination?

I propose you begin to focus less on the cost of your products and more on how they are used at home.

THE NEXT BIG THING—UNBUNDLING

We see it at Sam's Club and Costco, and we are about to see it everywhere! Sam's sells products for which there is no useful service component. We don't need service with a drum of detergent or a bale of TP. And there are products you sell that the consumer may want to purchase with the service charged removed.

Unbundled services are the basis of a cafeteria. How can they become the basis of your operation? How can you allow your customer to pick and choose cafeteria-style? Would you be embarrassed to charge for service now already included in your price? Would your customers be willing to pay your "real" price for service, once they have seen the cost of the product unbundled from the offer?

"I haven't had a bad airline meal since they stopped serving them." Today, dinner flights on mainstream airlines are far and few between. I say, good! The airlines were just trying to cut costs. They had no idea they were wrestling with a fundamental of the marketplace. The airlines weren't thinking; they were reacting. It was the consumer, through price resistance, who was messing with the proposition, saying, "Instead of providing me with a crummy meal and padding the fare, why not let me decide where, when, and what's for dinner and pass along the savings?"

Today, at almost any airport, you can get real food served by folks for whom food service is a core competency. This is a prime example of one service (providing a meal) being unbundled from another (air transportation).

SERVICE EFFICIENCY

In the near future, it won't be price or quality that separates the winners from the losers. It will be service efficiency. Essentially, this is what happened when highly unionized airline caterers gave way to minimum wage, tipped employees at the Chili's in the airport terminal.

The search for service efficiency is what caused high-priced auto dealership mechanics to be displaced by lower-paid, ten-minute lube joint grease monkeys. It's also the reason why a call to Sprint gets you placed on hold, while your connection drifts through cyberspace and lands in New Delhi.

When quality at a value price becomes the rule rather than the exception, the final frontier of competition will be service efficiency. How can you, as an industry, lower the cost of service?

TREND: THE GROWING POWER OF BRANDS

"There is no future in competing on price.
Relationships will once again reign supreme."
T. SCOTT GROSS

Although we talk about the demise of customer loyalty to a particular retailer, there is continuing power in brand loyalty. This is especially true when consumer brands are endorsed by athletes, actors, and other high-profile people. How else can you explain the premium willingly paid for the privilege of wearing Tommy Hilfiger in three-inch letters down the leg of a jogging suit, or Old Navy emblazoned across the chest of an otherwise unremarkable T-shirt?

Old Navy? Isn't that a retailer? Yes, and it is also a brand. I doubt that Old Navy customers are nearly as loyal to Old Navy, the store, as they are to Old Navy, the cool person's brand. Even the loyalty isn't to the brand, as much as it is to all the other people who wear Old Navy. Take Old Navy off the front of the shirt and put it on the tag inside, and

Old Navy would have to compete on price and may have trouble finding shelf space at Target. Can you imagine a line of casual sportswear with Wal-Mart stamped across the chest? Give me a break!

Go to Sporty's. Sit in the Need for Speed room. Check out the posters, and you'll see that fans are far more loyal to NASCAR drivers than the brand logos plastered across the hoods of their cars. The sponsors can only hope that some of that loyalty will translate to top-of-mind awareness and eventually a sale.

In the future, the power of the brand may be the only difference between commodity and luxury.

Commodities have little value beyond function. Premium brands (luxuries) are about feelings. Today's consumer is an educated buyer, who well understands the difference between the product and the system that delivered it. Commodities they want cheap and easy. There's no need to wrap an experience around a commodity. I don't want to pay for a commodity experience, and besides, I won't want to wait on it if it is free!

But the same individual who drives 15 miles to save a buck on a bale of TP will do that driving a $50,000 Lincoln Navigator SUV (which is an expensive way to say Ford Expedition, but for the extra bucks you feel better about both your purchase and yourself. Now there's an experience, a brand worth paying for!).

Dog food, which ought to be a commodity, is often sold as a premium brand. Go to PetSmart and watch which bags get carried to the 4Runner. I'd guess half the bags will be premium brands. Why? Because commodities are about function (feeding the dog), while brands are about feelings (loving the family pet).

In the future, brands will become more important, but not in the way we see them today in the mass markets. Mass marketing is losing steam. It's dying, if not already dead. In the future, local brands, call them MicroBrands, will matter most. MicroBrands will target customers, not as a market but as unique individuals with unique expectations, needs, and profit potential. It's almost like a return to the good old days, and that's disruptive in the nicest way!

COMPETING ON PRICE

The headline read, "Pricing Power Is Dead." My gut reaction was nonsense! Price *is* a huge deal. And then I read on and realized that the author was dead-on. Price is a huge deal, and the idea of price isn't what is dying. It's pricing power that is dying.

I think I'll write a novel where the bad guys are a syndicate of major retailers who conspire to knock out the Internet. First, they resort to violence, but even corporate-funded terrorism fails because the phone companies haven't been cut in on the deal. Finally, the bad guys will give up on violence and write a check to Congress. The Internet gets taxed until it is dead, and retailers everywhere rejoice.

How can you compete on price when a lower price is but a few clicks away?

We all have stories. Last week our son, Rod, who owns a car stereo and alarm shop, tipped a waiter $20 on an $8 tab. The waiter had told our son that he planned to buy a new car stereo and asked if he could get a good deal. "Absolutely! If I'm not there, tell them I sent you, and we'll give you the best deal in town." He should have said "best deal on the Internet," because that's exactly where the waiter made his purchase on a boatload of gray market car stereo equipment. (But he did apply the $20 toward the installation fees—of course, after asking for a deal.)

In some respects, the Internet is leading a fast race to the bottom, as margins in manufacturing and retailing alike get slimmer and slimmer. Buying direct for many items may eventually wipe out distribution channels that have been in place for decades or longer. If there is good news, it is that new structures will take their place. We'll just have to learn to live with them.

WHAT TO DO?

When the angel with the blue, blue eyes asks, "Pops, will you take us to the circus?" there really is no debate. Add in the fact that the owner of the voice is only six years old and that Pops is pronounced in three south Texas syllables, and the answer is a foregone "Yes, Princess, we'll all go to the circus." Buns and the county ag barn aren't normally on a collision course, but for one night my city girl will hold her nose and wait for the first unwelcome whiff of tiger, elephant, and, of course, ponies.

We bought our tickets, were thanked by several fez-wearing Shriners, and stepped inside to the sound of numerous high-pitched voices shouting "sne cerns" (snow cones) in an accent I couldn't begin to place. Other voices touted cotton candy (pink or blue), popcorn, and a plethora of stuff your mom wouldn't let you have even *after* dinner. Lucky for the Princess and Big Guy, we aren't mom and dad. We're Pops and Granny Buns, and besides, how often does the circus come to town?

We rode the elephant and then the ponies. Big Guy held a python and posed for a six-dollar photo. By the time the ringmaster took his place in the spotlight, the Princess had already devoured a whirl of cotton candy as big as a 60's bouffant hairdo and as blue as the eyes that peeked over the top.

The circus was small but wonderful, with three rings and a cage for the tigers, Chinese acrobats, jugglers, and a duo of clowns who communicated loudly through shrill-noted whistles. The tiger act was wonderful, the elephant was amazing, but as with kids everywhere, it was the whistling clowns that drew the most laughter and approving applause. The "children of all ages" were totally drawn into the moment, and that's exactly where we were when the ringmaster brought the show to a sudden halt saying, "I want to stop for just a moment. I've noticed that many of our circus friends are enjoying the circus whistles and would probably like a chance to take one home. We're going to make a special offer for tonight's performance only."

Oh, no, here it comes! I thought. Turning to the clowns, he asked, "What would our audience expect to pay for a real circus whistle just like the ones you're using tonight?" The clowns whistled a response that the ringmaster interpreted, "Ten dollars? Maybe some other night, but not for this audience!"

More whistling. "Did you say five dollars? Not tonight!"

Then there was whistling that could only be interpreted as puzzled. I was totally into the moment, expecting the Princess whose blue eyes had grown to saucer-size to ask, "Pops, what are they saying?" But the Princess needed no help at all interpreting whistle-ese.

"No, boys and girls! Tonight and only tonight you can take home an official circus clown whistle for just two dollars! Everyone who wants to take home an official circus whistle, raise your hand." A forest of small hands shot into the air, some still holding their four-dollar cotton candy. "Keep your hands up, folks, and our circus representatives will come to you as long as our limited supplies last."

And that was that. There was no saying "no." No attempt to explain the concept of rip-off. No economics lesson about plastic whistles made in China. No quibbling over two dollars. There were just two official circus whistles and the prospect of hearing whistle-talk all the way home to Mom and Dad.

How did that happen? How was a guy who saw the whole thing coming caught standing in the bleachers fishing a few more greenbacks from his jeans? Experience. We hadn't bought three laps on a pony or a chance to mount a prodigious pachyderm. At least I didn't. I bought *the magic* of walking beside the pony with a Princess who would only be six once. I bought a memory of Big Guy hoisting a 30-pound python and looking smug, as only a sixth grader can look. I bought the experience.

We'll save you the trouble of backing up a chapter or two to remind you of the five things most important to a retail customer.

Number one: We want friendly, caring staff.

Number two: We want knowledgeable, helpful staff.

A fair price is number three on the list, and it's not even a close number three. Friendly weighed in at 41.4 percent. Knowledgeable was 27.0 percent. In distant third place at 18.3 percent was fair price, yet this is the one that gets all the attention.

In the second quarter of 2004, Neiman Marcus reported that its strong earnings were due in part to full-price selling. While the rest of the world was waiting for the sound of another price going down, Neiman Marcus was listening to the gentle tune that goes cha-ching! (Anybody can give away product. It takes brains to sell it.) Neiman Marcus essentially tells the market, "We have what you want, the way you want it, and you're going to love the experience."

Back to our list, number four is merchandise that is organized and easy to find, 8.8 percent, and number five is speedy and accurate checkout, 4.5 percent.

At least four of the five top customer satisfiers have to do with the experience of shopping and buying. You can argue that price is or at least can be part of the experience. As anecdotal proof, I offer a look at a couple of national pizza chains where the marketing premise is summed up in a single word—cheap. I've heard many parents say, "We order that pizza for the kids and their friends and order our pizza from another place."

In the coming years, as price edges lower while quality climbs higher, experience will be the point of difference. And that's where we meet Fitch:RPA, specialists in retail experience. Fitch:RPA is a division of Fitch, a global, multidisciplinary design firm with over 550 associates in 18 studios in 11 countries. Fitch, a WPP company, enacts a distinct four-step process, executed by 17 disciplines for the last 45 years in more than 50 countries and with over 2,200 brands.

Fitch:RPA bills itself as a "Retail Experience Agency," a position that says right up front that something different is about to happen. It's not a design service where you just get advice on fixtures and color pallets. Retail experience is not the usual matter of creating marketing materials, although both can be a part of the deliverable.

Too often, retailers start with a store layout as a given; it's the premise or starting point. Creating an effective retail experience—one that sells product—begins with the customer and requires intense and effective listening. Says Mike Bills, managing director of Fitch:RPA: "The goal is to create consumer-centric experiences that transcend mere aesthetics and touch consumers at the point of interaction. Every customer interaction is important, including how a consumer reacts to and interacts with environment, product, packaging, corporate identity, collateral, events, and digital designs. Across these and brand touch-points, we create real, tangible experiences that invite and demand interaction and distinct moments that drive repeat, destination visits and uses."

To create a world-class retail experience, we have to give top consideration to customer needs ". . . instead of decorating around existing operational parameters," adds Bills. Price, selection, goods, and services are no longer the only purchase triggers. (They probably never were; we just thought they were.) Smart retailers who encourage customers to talk and then listen and act on what they hear will create experiences that build long-term brand affinity and loyalty, before, during, and after a purchase.

REALLY?

Are we really on our way to an experience economy? We decided to perform a simple test to see if industry is really looking forward or simply clinging to the past while waiting for someone else to take the first step. The question was simple: What one social movement, technological advance, legislative action, or economic event is likely to have the greatest impact on your industry in the coming five to ten years? That's pretty straightforward, and so were the answers. The majority answered, "Huh?" It turns out that too few retail thinkers are thinking further than, say, next Friday.

Think of all the "what ifs" that could totally turn your business upside-down. Consider the book you are holding. Only a few years ago, books online or available via CD-ROM were thought to be the beginning of the end of the publishing industry. True, book sales aren't what they could be, and reading among young people is at an all-time low, but the forecasts of imminent doom were more than a tad premature. In spite of having rather poor vision, at least someone was looking to the future. (By the way, why do you think e-books have been so poorly received? It turns out that we like to highlight and dog-ear. We like the feel of a book. We like to tuck books in our carry-on and leave them in the bathroom. We like the experience of a book. E-books will succeed once the rest of the experience, that part that lies outside the printed word, becomes part of the package.)

Here's what the National Automobile Dealers Association (NADA) gave us as its preview of the future of the auto business. How about some really huge numbers to get us started? In 2002 (the most recent figures available), there were 135,920,677 passenger cars on the road in the United States. Add in 92,938,587 trucks and buses and you have a traffic jam of 228,859,264 vehicles on the road. And that's just in this country!

The auto industry is huge with a capital H. The average new-vehicle dealership sales are a healthy $32.3 million, and total sales for the industry are pushing $700 billion! When the auto industry makes a change, you can be certain that the entire economy will follow right along.

We asked Paul Taylor, chief economist for NADA, what was on the horizon. Surprisingly, we got nearly the same answer that we heard from a leading manufacturer of airline flight controls while working on another project in 2003. In the very near future, expect to see cars (and airplanes) that diagnose themselves and report to their owners or perhaps even directly to the technician. Onboard diagnostics can advise the owner to open the communications channel to the dealership, where final diagnosis can be made and parts ordered even before the vehicle hits the service drive.

Service will be more efficient, and cars no doubt will last longer. But won't cars that last longer hurt sales in the long term? Taylor seems to think not, saying that longer-lasting vehicles may be seen as a better value by the consumer.

Also on the horizon is a potential sea change that will ripple through the economy, not just in the West but the entire world, that will have a tremendous impact on the environment. We're talking about hydrogen-powered vehicles, whose by-product of combustion is nothing but plain old H_2O. The greatest stumbling block is not the lack of infrastructure, although that's a big one. The problem is that hydrogen, while found abundantly in things as common as seawater, is extremely expensive to produce.

The industry is not waiting on a technological breakthrough in the cost of producing hydrogen. Fuel cell technology continues to be refined and other energy-saving technologies like using braking to recapture energy are showing up in the hybrid vehicles that have become increasingly popular. Taylor knows his stuff, but I am willing to bet the evolution of the auto industry will have as much or more to do with the experience of buying and owning a vehicle as it will with power plant and maintenance technology.

Our research consistently said consumers can't stand the thought of shopping for a vehicle. A search of the world-famous Clusterizer for the parameters "car sales" brought up these turnoffs on the first page alone:

- "Pushy salespeople/car dealers offend"
- "Being approached and hounded by sales associates at car dealerships"
- "Pushy salespeople/car dealerships, take your pick"
- "Salespeople following you around. The biggest offenders are car salesmen."

That explains the success of Santa Fe auto consultant Fred Vang, who makes a living matching people with the cars they want to buy. One call to Fred and a bit of pleasant conversation followed by a couple dozen questions about how, where, and even why you drive, is all it takes to have the car of your dreams delivered to your home or office without once having to endure that happy horse manure about having to "check with the sales manager."

Technology may change the industry, but it may be that poor buying service experiences may kill it first!

Another huge segment of our economy that, in many respects, tracks parallel to the auto industry is the lodging industry. America is dotted with hotels and motels, a surprisingly large number of which are mom-and-pop operations, many totally independent. The American Hotel & Lodging Association sent us this response: "Thank you for contacting us. To answer your question, the health of the U.S. economy is closely tied to the nation's hotel industry; conversely, the national economy is the largest factor affecting the lodging sector. Barring major disruptive events, we anticipate that this will continue to be the case in coming years."

From their Web site, we lifted:

While external factors such as rising interest rates, inconsistency in the overall economic recovery, the Presidential election, the Iraq war, security, and world affairs continue to inspire caution, they no longer appear to be driving the course of the lodging sector. To a growing extent, the lodging industry and its customers are incorporating these concerns into—but not letting them dictate—business. We believe this trend will continue, barring major disruptive events.

Concerns about safety and convenience continue to affect lodging demand. However, Americans have increasingly followed advice from the Department of Homeland Security to go forward with travel plans, gather with family and friends, and continue to enjoy their lives and freedom.

Ah, so experience has come to include feelings about safety! And what about the soon-to-be-realized self check-in, where all you do is swipe your credit card at the lobby kiosk, verify your room preference, and you're on your way? Just use your credit card as the room key. The industry has done so poorly at making check-in a welcoming, positive experience that travelers would just as soon skip it and say "good-night" to a machine.

Know it or like it or not, retailing is and will always be about the experience.

TRAVEL AND TOURISM

We asked National Tour Association President Hank Phillips, CTP, to gaze into the crystal ball and tell us the single most important idea, technology, regulation, or social movement likely to impact the tour industry in the coming five to ten years. His answer was a sign of the times—the freedom to travel: "Recognizing that the travel industry is extremely resilient to change, and even to disruption, the one thing that could have the ultimate catastrophic impact on this industry would be the loss of freedom to travel. More specifically, the loss of freedom to travel because of reasons such as the fear of terrorism, the travel restrictions brought on by terrorism, or the economic upheavals resulting in travel not being affordable to the masses."

HEALTH CARE

A huge health care issue revolves around how to provide it and who will pay for it. There is a push to get more of the price paid by the consumer with the possibilities of unimagined ramifications, as patients take a greater role in what is purchased and how to find it.

The doctor orders an expensive MRI and, instead of an already steep copay of $300, the tab runs to $600. Is the patient going to refuse? Will the insurance company insist in order to prevent even greater expenses that may crop up later if undetected now? And what about the potential for giant increases in bad debt? Is there anyone who doesn't know that hospitals cannot refuse emergency care and that, at the drop of a hat, will forgive unpaid bills?

Perhaps the biggest issue—and it's a matter of ethics—will come to the fore as the science of genomics moves from the laboratory to the exam room. Will we refuse to hire and insure an individual who has a gene that is a precursor to cancer? If I can predict at your birth that you will likely die early of leukemia, will I want to spend for your education?

In America, we are both blessed and cursed by the availability of marvelous new medical technology. Now, how do we pay for it? Will there be the have and have-not health care organizations based on availability of capital? If we say we must listen when customers talk, then don't we have to know *who* the customer is? Is the customer the patient, the physician, the insurance company, or the hospital? When the doctor owns the lab and orders yet another test, is he or she the customer or the provider?

These are huge issues that won't be easy to resolve. We should keep in mind that when everyone is talking, there will be no one to listen!

REAL ESTATE

Pamela J. O'Connor, president and CEO of The RELO® Network, http://www.RELO.com, gave us a forward look on real estate. She says three trends are shaping the business:

1. *Change in profile of the real estate agent.* As consumers rely more on the Internet to search for homes, and as some form of real estate services is offered through new channels like banks and Internet marketing companies, the real estate professional who survives and prospers will have to be more of a "knowledge" broker than housing tour guide. The real estate agent adds value by providing expertise on the market, the home, and transaction issues, and by facilitating and expediting the homebuying process. The average age of agents is high (mid-50s), so as these people leave the business, younger, more technology-savvy people are entering, many from other industries. They should affect

not only the profile of agents but also the employment model, with some real estate companies moving away from independent contractors to employees with employment benefits in order to compete for the best talent with other private sector industries. The health care crisis in this country plays into this.

2. *Potential decline in housing demand.* As baby boomers age, housing sales have actually increased rather than decreased, because so many have invested in second homes. Also, first-time buyers, many from among immigrants, have increased to create the largest housing boom ever. But going forward, as these boomers reach their 70s and 80s, they'll probably scale back to one or no homes (in favor of rental/assisted living). Those remaining in the market, even with continued growth in the immigrant homebuyer market, may not fully replace that demand, particularly in the higher-end price tiers.

3. *Housing affordability.* This is already a problem on both coasts of the country and could eliminate many first-time buyers from the market if it accelerates unchecked. However, if housing demand decreases, this could result in a downward trend in pricing, at least in some more volatile markets, which could help affordability.

Technology, demographics, and economics all will play an important role in how and where Americans live. But isn't it odd that the most successful Realtors sell not bricks and mortar but the experience of living in a new home?

ANY MESSAGE . . .

"Any message communicated in any way that
creates an expectation is an act of branding."
T. SCOTT GROSS

See the second edition of *Positively Outrageous Service* for a full explanation of MicroBranding. Fitch:RPA refers to these minimoments of branding as "Brand Touch-points." Says Bills:

Depending upon your perspective, Consumer Touch-points, or Brand Touch-points, are the names that Fitch:RPA gives to the various channels of communication that brand has at its disposal to communicate and interact with its consumers, or conversely, are *the points at which a consumer interacts with the brand.*" (Emphasis is mine.)

Touch-points include pre-purchase communication channels, such as print and broadcast advertising, and during purchase, channels such as online (Web sites, e-mail communication), marketing communication (including rotos, circulars, direct mail), packaging corporate identities, in-store environments (including merchandising, store design, visual communication), and post-purchase touch-points including packaging and customer service.

Modern technology, in particular the Internet, makes possible the two-way communication, a dialogue between the brand and the consumer, and moves control of the conversation and, therefore, control of the brand closer to the consumer. Says Bills, "Finally, this conversation must constantly seek to deliver on the brand promise and positioning that is first established in the initial touch-points (advertising)."

For well-managed brands, experience is now in the hands of the consumer. On a macro scale, when one of our Sporty's guests asks for a change of the television channel, we are fond of handing over the remote control and saying, "This is America; you're at Sporty's. Do what you want"; or in other words, "Take control of your experience." You will see this more and more on a larger scale and in more settings as businesses learn to listen when customers talk.

IF A MAN SPEAKS IN A FOREST . . .

Buns plopped one of her women's magazines on my desk and stood looking over my shoulder, grinning as I read: "If a man speaks in a forest and there is no woman there to hear . . . is he still wrong?" She seemed to think he would be. Funny or not, the comment makes a good point. If you do something for a customer and the customer doesn't know it, did you really do it? And if that were an accurate reflection of the situation, would it not add to the cost but not add to the value?

Or how about: "If a customer has an unresolved need and the retailer doesn't know about it, which goes away, the need or the customer?" Referring to our top-five customer wants, it's plain that our job is to create an experience. Experience is always emotional. So how do we create an emotional connection?

Again from Mike Bills of Fitch:RPA:

We believe that the single, most significant challenge facing retailers today is to connect with consumers on an emotional level. After decades of focusing on operational efficiency, wringing every last dime of profitability out of their businesses, retailers are slowly waking up to the fact that they are no longer in control of the purchase process. Like the proliferation of choices in television, today's retail landscape is littered with choices . . . .

Over the last 10 to 20 years . . . the market has undergone massive change, which on the surface appears to have been subtle, unrelated, and less significant than in reality. The advent of the Internet, the success of cataloguers in becoming true multi-channel retailers, the explosion of micro-marketed media choices, the diminishing reach of traditional broadcast advertising, the increase in cross-channel shopping by consumers of all demographics, and the ongoing shrinking of the middle class and economic polarization are just a few of the societal and retail industry shifts that have conspired to dramatically change the competitive landscape . . . .

It should not be surprising then that these consumers are choosing to purchase from retailers who support and fulfill their EMOTIONAL needs and desires rather than merely their logical, more rational needs of convenience, location, low prices, and selection—criteria that have defined the value proposition of the majority of retailers over the last 30 years. Which is not to say that low prices, convenience, and selection aren't vital. Wal-Mart has proven that this is a winning strategy. So successful of a strategy, in fact, that Wal-Mart now owns this value proposition outright. Consumers have voted with their pocketbooks and wallets that in the absence of an emotionally fulfilling experience at retail, these base-level, rational needs and the emotional connection to those will suffice.

And retailers took notice in lemming-like fashion, imitating the operationally centric tactics of Wal-Mart across the board. The result, however, has been that this approach plays directly into Wal-Mart's hand rather than strengthening competitors' positions. Category killers who offer few discernable differences from Wal-Mart are learning the hard way that imitation may be the best form of flattery but is definitely not the best strategy for remaining competitive against Wal-Mart . . . .

For most all retailers other than Wal-Mart, therefore, it is vital to their survival and continued success that they redefine their value proposition to include an emotional resonance with their target consumer. A resonance that promotes long-term brand affinity and loyalty. In other words, this is about changing the game, not imitating the leader. If a toy retailer offers little more than the same toys at higher prices than Wal-Mart offers, why shop them? The same holds true [for] housewares, apparel, pet supplies, etc. . . .

Making the emotional tangible requires a consumer-centric focus rather than an operationally focused emphasis. It is about creating an electronics store specifically geared toward women and how they purchase electronics rather than designing a home theater store. It is about creating a destination for mom and her child that creates and encourages all of the activities and emotional triggers that drive repeat destination visits with longer dwell time instead of "decorating" a new toy store concept. It is about designing a home copier that is specifically geared toward the stay-at-home mom and working mom, focusing on the shapes, forms, functions, and sensibilities that she recognizes as similar to home appliances and that are important to her rather than merely designing a solution for a particular retail channel or certain price point.

CREATING DIFFERENTIATED CONSUMER-CENTRIC EXPERIENCES

The following information was provided by Mike Bills at Fitch:RPA:

1. **Accept that your consumer, not you, is in control.** With very few exceptions, the consumer has innumerable choices in acquiring either exactly the same, or very similar, products that you create and/or sell. The choice is no longer merely about minimizing cost and maximizing efficiency, but also about pleasing and even surpassing the expectations and desires of today's multichannel shopper, who has more choices than ever. Acceptance will allow you to focus on what really matters, regardless of what Wall Street might be telling you. Also recognize that control is a relative desire, often served by perception more than re-

ality. For example, with the plethora of choices often comes confusion and indecision, inducing an overwhelming "out of control" emotion. One resolution to enhance the perception of "control," and thus the consumer's reality of it, is for retailers to become an editor of choice. Thus, often, less can be more.

2. Really get to know your target consumer. Get to the heart of understanding who your target consumer is both in market size and potential, and, more important, what drives and motivates consumers' interest or potential interest in your products and services. Don't just observe their shopping preferences and buying habits regarding frequency, convenience, price points, and selection, but also explore their deep, emotional desires relating to your offer—wants versus needs, tastes versus habits, emotional interests versus rational, pragmatic choices.

3. Invert your development process to begin with the consumer. Develop products and formats based on what consumers want and need versus residual output from R&D that the organization wants to find a use for.

4. Understand and play to your strengths. Embrace your core capabilities and competitive differences and emphasize your strengths. Determine the values your brand truly believes in and can support and back up—not what the competition is doing, but what your company does best and how your offer can enhance the lives of your consumer. Most critical, do not promise what you cannot deliver. The market sets base-level expectations. If you promise above those, be prepared and capable of delivering on the expectations that you set. It is better to surprise and delight than to disappoint.

5. Don't keep your positioning a secret. Talk to consumers directly and consistently about what makes you truly different and best at something that your competitors can't do better.

6. Let go of your weaknesses. Accept that on some fronts the competition is better, stronger, and more proficient and, as a result, may have a permanent lead on you. This doesn't mean not to try and improve and compete in these areas. It means finding a niche and a particular target consumer that values your strengths over those of your competitors.

7. Force organizational innovation. This is not about the CEO's perspective. This is about a wake-up call to your company, preferably when you are doing well, so you can continue to ideate, test, and stay ahead of the competition. Instill a sensibility of innovation among your employees. Remember, innovation should be tested constantly, and missteps won't hurt the bottom line because you won't roll it out until it works.

8. Don't confuse design with decorating or an experience with entertainment. Making your store or product more visually appealing and easier to use or shop is important but provides only a temporary competitive advantage. Identifying, communicating, and encouraging interactive experiences between your consumer and your product or store environment, on the other hand, can provide a long-term competitive advantage. And remember, experiential design is an interactive experience, not passive entertainment that a consumer watches. Interactive experiences invite repeat patronage; passive entertainment is over the minute the consumer has "seen the show."

9. Stop decorating around existing operational parameters. Consumers don't care about how much product you lose to theft. Nor do they care that product is positioned in a particular department due to lower placement costs. They also don't care that a particular product function was cheaper to develop than if you'd given them the function they wanted. Instead, they want what they want, and they'll get it from whoever gives it to them in the manner they insist on. The first to do so stands a far greater chance of being rewarded with long-term loyalty and financial success.

10. Create compelling retail experiences. Emulate experience leaders. If you are a pet supply retailer, offer grooming and obedience school. If you're a toy retailer, test party concepts that mom and child both desire. Electronics? Offer videotaped instructions of installation of their purchase. DIY? Offer meaningful classes in home improvement within an environment that facilitates both awareness and learning. Furniture store? Provide a playground environment with child supervision. If it puts more product in the average basket, increases dwell time, increases average ticket, steals market share, and begins to build loyalty, then there will be a way to operationalize the solution and minimize increases to staff costs. But if you don't, you may never know and are opening yourself up to the possibility that your competition will implement these or other ideas that emphasize their strengths and positioning.

11. Stay on top and start early. Early warning signs are often missed by retailers mired in the day-to-day, short-term myopia created by operational efficiencies and Wall Street. More often than not, retailers try to make paradigm-shifting decisions too late. And while they still manage to create new and differentiating decisions, they no longer have the time to allow for the ideas to manifest with consumers and produce the desired impact. Thus, we find that the retailer ends up "Killing the Cure^{SM}" and not saving the ship.

THE GRAND SLAM

Maybe Denny's is a good analogy for listening to customers. I worked my way through college by cooking at Denny's. The 6 AM breakfast shift was my favorite. It seemed we had more regulars at breakfast at Denny's than for any other day-part. I liked the early-morning friendly faces, and I liked that there was so little mystery about what our customers wanted.

It didn't really matter what they asked for; we knew what they wanted. Take the lady who always ordered her eggs scrambled well done but not dry. Sports fans, I hate to tell you this, but well done is, by definition, dry. What she really wanted were medium scrambled eggs that we then chopped into a gazillion pieces so they would look, but not taste, like the nasty eggs her mother cooked for her.

And there was the fellow who wanted his eggs "up over easy." Up? No problem. Over easy? Piece of cake. But up over easy, what the heck is that? We finally figured he wanted his eggs with cooked whites, yet runny yoke. No problem up (if you know the trick) or over easy; either one will do the job. But until I walked around the counter and listened while the customer talked, all the guessing in the world wouldn't have cooked those eggs the way he wanted.

Creating a retail experience requires proactive listening, which means more than asking the right questions. It includes helping customers see possibilities that may expand their answers. You could, for example, ask customers what they want, a good question for sure. But what if you asked not just what they wanted but also ask what they would love? What you want deals with expectations. What you love is all about possibilities as yet unconsidered.

You want to ask, "What kind of shopping experience would change your opinions about yourself? What would make you feel smarter or perhaps more stylish?" Understand that what consumers say may be different from what they do and think. Customers may have trouble telling you what they will be doing long term, because they base their answers on what they know. Asking "What is your ideal experience?" may yield an answer that does not extrapolate to a new idea of what will turn them on.

The goal is to get inside the consumer's head to discover emotional triggers. For example, Target chose as its model customer the upscale suburban soccer mom and then set out to create an experience that would make this cohort say wow. Now they own the position of "fashion for less."

Chico's chose as its target a market one that is older, larger, and more upscale. Want to make a large consumer feel good about herself? Offer just three sizes: 1, 2, and 3! Liz Claiborne did much the same when she changed regular size 12 to a Liz Claiborne size 8 and, even though women knew, it still felt good.

Brand execution should focus on the creation of the experience perfectly matched to the target market. Begin by carefully defining the target market and then build the experience around it. Forget convention. Let operations take a back seat. Prepare to listen, not just for expectations but also for feelings and possibilities, and keep listening every day.

And if you are a big box discounter, beware the independent shop keeper who is there to listen and react nearly instantly when customers talk!

For more information, visit http://www.whencustomerstalk.com.

10

CLICHÉ OR REALITY?

The Big Guy (our grandson) had discovered his face. He was about eight and right in the middle of the gross-out age. First, he pulled down the skin right beneath his eyes. Then he pushed his nose up, while smacking his rendition of fish lips. For a finale, he somehow managed to fold his earlobe so that it tucked neatly into his ear.

I knew what was next and headed him off at the pass saying, "Big Guy, if you cross your eyes, they might . . ." You can finish the sentence, I am sure. It's one of those myths we all learn while growing up. We've all tested it, crossing our eyes just a little bit and then a little bit further, until we discovered that they didn't really get stuck.

If we can risk getting our eyeballs permanently stuck, why do we continue to live with retail myths and clichés without so much as a quick test? We've taken the most common retail myths and put them to the test. Here's what we discovered.

CUSTOMERS REALLY WON'T PAY MORE FOR QUALITY AND SERVICE

Quality is expected and service is considered part of the deal. And it's getting worse, not better.

FIGURE 10.1 *Women's Clothes–Motivated to Deal!*

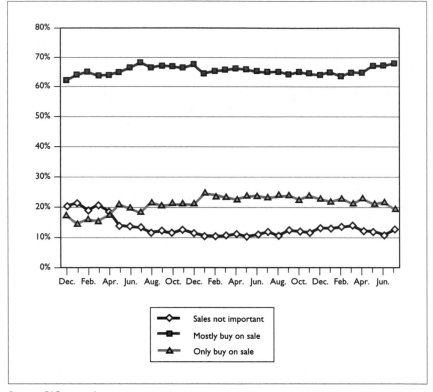

Source: BIGresearch.

Check out the graph in Figure 10.1. The data involves shopping for women's clothes and accessories, so we can expect the results to be different for other segments and other industries. In other words, if we had a graph of how we shop for health care, it most likely would be different. A graph of how we might select a physician for neurosurgery might look even more different.

The top line of the graph represents the percentage of customers who buy women's clothes mostly when they are on sale. The far left data point is 62 percent; the most recent data point is 67.8 percent. In the past three or so years, more than 1 of 20 shoppers has switched to the "I buy mostly on sale" group. Where did they come from?

They came either from the "Sales not important" or the "Only buy on sale" groups. Would you want to make a friendly wager before we go on? Look at the "Only buy on sale" line. These are the folks who know that if they outwait the retailer, they are going to get that suede jacket at 40 percent off. They used to be under 20 percent (that's one in five!)

of the shopping population, and, according to our latest sample, they still are.

But here's the big one, the bottom line has changed dramatically. This is the group that buys what they want, when they want it, and money isn't the deciding factor. They used to account for one in five shoppers in the category. They were the "They've got it, I want it now" group. If money was an object, it certainly wasn't much of an object. Look at the chart! Some of the "Mostly buy on sale" group joined the "Only buy on sale" group. But a whole lot of folks from the "Sales not important" community changed their tune and joined the "Mostly buy on sale" folks.

Price became an issue.

The "Sales not important" group fell from 21.3 percent of the shoppers in the category to 12.5 percent (up from a low of 10.4 percent). That's a decline of 41 percent! Thinking about your product or service, if 41 percent of the folks willing to pay for the experience suddenly became more price sensitive, what would you do?

Customers will pay for the service experience and quality, just not like they used to!

Look at consumer electronics as an example. As you can see from Figure 10.2, consumers with annual incomes of $150,000 and more are half again (46 percent) more likely to pay for service as a consumer making $30,000, for whom price gets the edge (15.9 percent).

Let's try an example on how to read this chart. All of the respondents with an income in excess of $150,000 make up 1.5 percent of the sample. But of all the respondents who said service was most important to them, 2.2 percent have incomes in excess of $150,000.

Here's another example. Folks making around $30,000 accounted for 15.8 percent of the survey population. Looking one column to the right, we see that this same group puts a slightly higher premium on price (15.9 percent) and are not as concerned about selection (15.3 percent).

Choosing price, selection, or quality as your main reason for selecting a retailer does not imply that the other categories are not important. They're just not as important.

PEOPLE WILL PAY MORE FOR BETTER QUALITY

Like service, some people will pay more for quality, while others will not. It depends on the product. When we look at the reasons for shopping in the category of women's clothing (see Figure 10.3), we see that

FIGURE 10.2 *Reasons to Buy Electronics*

	All	Price	Selection	Location	Quality	Service
What is your gender?						
Male	48.1%	49.0%	50.9%	48.2%	51.9%	49.9%
Female	51.9%	51.0%	49.1%	51.8%	48.1%	50.1%
Total	100.0%	100.0%	100.0%	100.0%	100.0%	100.0%
Please tell us which age range you are in:						
18–24	13.0%	13.0%	12.9%	13.3%	15.5%	15.3%
25–34	18.1%	17.7%	18.2%	17.4%	18.4%	16.5%
35–44	21.8%	22.3%	21.5%	21.9%	20.7%	18.7%
45–54	18.3%	19.3%	18.7%	18.5%	18.0%	18.7%
55–64	11.8%	11.9%	12.0%	11.8%	11.5%	11.9%
65+	17.0%	15.9%	16.5%	17.2%	16.0%	18.9%
Total	100.0%	100.0%	100.0%	100.0%	100.0%	100.0%
Average Age	44.6	44.4	44.5	44.6	43.7	44.9
What is the annual total income of your household?						
Less than $15,000	12.5%	12.1%	10.9%	12.5%	12.4%	11.7%
$15,000 to $24,999	16.2%	15.1%	13.9%	14.0%	14.0%	13.7%
$25,000 to $34,999	15.8%	15.9%	15.3%	15.5%	15.7%	15.6%
$35,000 to $49,999	18.5%	18.3%	17.9%	18.3%	17.7%	17.1%
$50,000 to $74,999	21.9%	23.0%	24.4%	22.8%	23.7%	25.2%
$75,000 to $99,999	8.7%	9.0%	10.0%	8.7%	9.0%	9.2%
$100,000 to $149,999	4.8%	4.9%	5.7%	5.6%	5.3%	5.3%
$150,000 or more	1.5%	1.6%	1.9%	2.0%	2.2%	2.2%
Total	100.0%	100.0%	100.0%	100.0%	100.0%	100.0%
Average Income	$47,147	$48,011	$50,517	$48,942	$49,471	$50,159
What are the reasons you buy your electronics there? (Check all that apply.)						
Price	77.4%	100.0%	91.8%	90.1%	91.9%	90.7%
Selection	59.8%	71.0%	100.0%	75.9%	87.7%	86.7%
Location	46.5%	54.2%	59.0%	100.0%	62.3%	63.1%
Quality	40.5%	48.2%	59.4%	54.3%	100.0%	78.9%
Service	30.5%	35.8%	44.3%	41.5%	59.4%	100.0%
Good financing options	7.7%	9.1%	11.1%	10.1%	14.3%	16.2%
Knowledgeable salespeople	20.5%	23.9%	30.7%	26.5%	38.5%	47.8%
Have installation service for car, truck, and SUV	2.6%	3.3%	4.2%	4.0%	5.2%	6.2%
Have latest high-tech products	15.4%	18.1%	23.8%	19.6%	29.8%	31.6%
Other	3.5%	2.3%	2.3%	2.4%	2.2%	3.0%

The sum of the percent totals may be greater than 100 percent because the respondents can select more than one answer.

Source: BIGresearch, Consumer Intentions and Actions.

in the $150,000 and above group (1.8 percent), price (1.4 percent) isn't that big of a deal, but quality (2.3 percent) and service (2.4 percent) are very important. At this income level, we are dealing with a consumer who has little time, wants to get in and get out, and only wants to make this purchase once.

But how about mere mortals living in the real world, where household income is closer to $50,000? For this group, if there is a hot button at all, it's selection.

RETAIL IS 90 PERCENT LOCATION

As you can see from Figure 10.2 on reasons for shopping for consumer electronics, location is the third most mentioned reason—46.5 percent of the respondents cited location as a critical factor. But for women's clothes, location shows as important but not as important. It's still important and mentioned as number four, but only 39.3 percent mentioned it as important for women's clothes.

Again, the answer to our retail myth is, it depends on both the product and the individual consumer. This myth may exist because women shop for clothes at locations where they go for other reasons, or perhaps because retailers of women's clothes—with the exception of Wal-Mart—tend to be near other similar retailers in places such as malls and strip centers.

Loyalty isn't dead, but it's a lot tougher to achieve than you think.

While many worship at the altar of price, many are loyal brand followers. Think of any pro sports team. Last year, the LA Lakers were golden, and even when Kobe Bryant was dragged into court, the LA fans were just that—fans. Fans are so loyal to team brands that even when the team is losing, they still fly the team colors. The same is true with store brands and the big brands they carry.

There are many ways to be loyal that aren't obvious. You can be loyal to a standard of quality, a promise of fashion. You can be loyal to the other people who, like you, are flying the same colors or logos. You can be loyal to the people who staff the store. You can even be loyal to price.

You can be loyal to all of the above at the same time to a varying degree. Check out the preceding charts and look at the "reasons you buy there" sections and think of them as loyalty charts. Consumer loyalty can be defined as "resistance to change." Loyalty represents a composite of how well you are satisfying each of the components that make a great retailer great, and what it is that keeps your customer from becoming your competitor's customer.

FIGURE 10.3 *Reasons to Buy Women's Clothing*

	All	Price	Selection	Location	Quality	Service
What is your gender?						
Male	48.1%	32.2%	32.9%	34.9%	33.0%	37.6%
Female	51.9%	67.8%	67.1%	65.1%	67.0%	62.4%
Total	100.0%	100.0%	100.0%	100.0%	100.0%	100.0%
Please tell us which age range you are in:						
18–24	13.0%	10.6%	10.4%	11.8%	10.9%	10.3%
25–34	18.1%	17.6%	16.8%	16.7%	15.8%	14.0%
35–44	21.8%	22.1%	20.4%	20.1%	20.0%	17.4%
45–54	18.3%	18.8%	18.4%	19.0%	17.4%	16.0%
55–64	11.8%	12.8%	13.4%	12.9%	14.0%	15.9%
65+	17.0%	18.1%	20.6%	19.5%	21.8%	26.4%
Total	100.0%	100.0%	100.0%	100.0%	100.0%	100.0%
Average Age	44.6	45.7	46.6	46.0	47.0	48.9
What is the annual total income of your household?						
Less than $15,000	12.4%	11.3%	10.0%	11.5%	10.5%	11.1%
$15,000 to $24,999	16.2%	15.8%	14.9%	15.4%	13.8%	16.4%
$25,000 to $34,999	15.8%	16.7%	15.5%	16.9%	16.1%	16.5%
$35,000 to $49,999	19.9%	20.6%	20.1%	19.8%	19.7%	20.9%
$50,000 to $74,999	20.1%	20.3%	21.6%	20.9%	21.5%	19.0%
$75,000 to $99,999	8.5%	9.0%	9.8%	8.8%	10.1%	8.6%
$100,000 to $149,999	5.3%	4.9%	6.1%	5.2%	6.0%	5.2%
$150,000 or more	1.8%	1.4%	2.0%	1.5%	2.3%	2.4%
Total	100.0%	100.0%	100.0%	100.0%	100.0%	100.0%
Average Income	$47,475	$47,158	$50,351	$47,661	$50,821	$48,271
What are the reasons you buy your women's clothing there? (Check all that apply.)						
Price	61.4%	100.0%	85.6%	88.7%	83.0%	86.0%
Selection	53.1%	74.0%	100.0%	76.4%	87.0%	88.4%
Location	39.3%	56.7%	56.6%	100.0%	58.1%	71.0%
Quality	39.6%	53.5%	64.9%	58.5%	100.0%	84.5%
Service	17.3%	24.2%	28.8%	31.3%	37.0%	100.0%
Fashion ideas	11.7%	15.3%	19.8%	17.9%	23.9%	30.4%
Newest styles	13.0%	17.4%	22.3%	19.4%	26.0%	32.6%
Newest fabrics	5.0%	6.8%	8.9%	9.0%	11.7%	18.3%
Knowledgeable salespeople	7.8%	9.7%	13.0%	13.5%	16.8%	34.7%
Other	5.5%	4.0%	4.2%	3.5%	3.8%	4.5%

The sum of the percent totals may be greater than 100 percent because the respondents can select more than one answer.

Source: BIGresearch, Consumer Intentions and Actions.

This week, I began noticing a commercial for a line of clothes branded Route 66. The commercials are hip, the actor/models and their clothes are cute and sexy, and the music is just right, not rock and not hip. Just right. It had all the makings of a killer brand. Then, in the last few seconds, you discover you can only get Route 66 at Kmart, the last place you would look for hip, cute, or sexy.

The big question is, Will consumers who regard themselves as hip, cute, and sexy want the association with Kmart? If the ads get them through the door, will the other elements of loyalty be strong enough to make them buy and buy again?

Looking down the clothing aisle, when we ask for a response to, "When buying clothes, familiar labels are important to me," since January 2002, between 29 and 38 percent have said yes.

There is interesting research by Werner Reinartz and V. Kumar (*Harvard Business Review*, 2002), because it reveals that doing everything just right as a retailer or servic-ustomers are less costly to serve. They know what they want and require little sales time and product training. And, because they are loyal, they will wait longer and pay more. It ain't necessarily so.

Reinartz and Kumar were unable to find significant evidence that loyal customers are in fact cheaper to serve or willing to pay more. In fact, just the opposite seemed to be the case. Long-term customers were presumed to be loyal customers, but guess what? Because they were such long-term customers, they considered themselves as worthy of a deal. They knew their value to the company and frequently relied on their status to demand lower prices and better service.

Perhaps better than focusing on customer loyalty is the idea of looking at customer profitability. On a macro level, at Sporty's, we are constantly hammered to put out point-of-purchase materials promoting special prices on drinks and appetizers. Why? Why would you say to a customer, who is already in your business with the intention to buy (few restaurant guests say, "no thanks, just looking), "Now that you are here, there's really no need to pay full price." That's an express method for turning a profitable transaction into a marginally profitable transaction.

You may be surprised to discover that your happy hour regular is not nearly as profitable as the minister from the church around the corner who pops in occasionally with a church bus filled with hungry choir members. Which one should you spend time and money to court? The coupon shopper in your store this week will be down the street next week when your competitor's coupon hits the paper.

FIGURE 10.4 *Customer Loyalty by Shopping Category*

	Wal-Mart	JCPenney	Sears	Target	Kohl's
Women's clothing	29.3%	33.3%	5.9%	13.1%	55.1%
Men's clothing	35.2%	45.4%	11.7%	14.1%	58.2%
Children's clothing	26.9%	14.1%	4.4%	18.8%	23.3%
Shoes	26.2%	15.5%	6.8%	7.2%	28.2%
Linens/bedding	41.1%	46.8%	11.4%	22.8%	23.3%

Source: BIGresearch.

Reinartz and Kumar suggest that customers have different value to the enterprise, so it's only logical that they be treated differently. Customers likely to shop infrequently but who are a good match for the product should be treated well, but marketing should focus on getting them to buy more while they are in the store.

Customers who do not comfortably fit the product and price proposition (Reinartz and Kumar call them "strangers") are likely to be low-profit customers. Make a profit on every sale to this group and invest nothing in building a relationship.

Long-term customers who fit well with the product and price proposition are potentially your highest profitable customers. Love on these customers and fight hard to retain them. But long-term customers who buy only on price need an entirely different strategy. This group needs up-selling for higher sales as well as cross-selling for greater share of wallet. Otherwise, they will remain long-term, low-profit drains on margins, marketing, and manpower.

Share of wallet is the true product of loyalty. Loyal customers are most likely to shop in more departments more often.

Take, for example, clothing. Figure 10.4 shows that just because a customer shops a store most often for one category does not mean that this customer shops the same store for other categories.

Of those consumers who shop Wal-Mart most often for at least one category of merchandise, 29.3 percent shop Wal-Mart most often for women's clothing. Of those consumers who shop JCPenney most often for at least one category of merchandise, 45.4 percent shop JCPenney most often for men's clothing.

Loyalty can have a multitude of meanings, but in retailing rarely does loyalty translate to "I buy everything at. . . ." A customer may be loyal to a department but rarely 100 percent faithful to a store.

Figure 10.4 also shows that, at least in the categories selected, Kohl's has done a terrific job getting clothing shoppers to stay in the store when they are shopping for the entire family. Kohl's opportunity is in linens/bedding.

Wal-Mart and JCPenney are doing well at capturing linen/bedding customers.

Sears and Target have a few challenges, but that hardly brands them as losers. Obviously, Sears has other strong suits, and, without looking, we can safely say tools and appliances are right up there. But if you were a store owner or perhaps a shareholder, wouldn't you rather have a multidimensional operation? A greater share of customer gives you security in a changing market. If the bottom falls out of hard goods, Sears may be in serious trouble, because those shoppers aren't trained to come to the softer side of Sears.

The Greater the Selection, the Higher the Sales

Selection is consistently the number two reason, following price as the number one reason for shopping.

Customers Are Price Sensitive

Customers have learned to separate the product from the distribution system, which makes them very price sensitive when purchasing items with little or no service component, such as detergent, soft drinks, or paper towels. These are viewed as commodities, and price really is important. And older people are more price sensitive about consumables and apparel.

TELEVISION NO LONGER WORKS AS A SOLE MARKETING MEDIUM

There's television, and then there is cable. Some predicted that cable would be the downfall of network TV and, to a certain extent, it has been. Cable gobbled up a considerable chunk of former network TV viewers. This was especially critical at a time when young adults were finding other things to do with their time besides watch the tube.

Recently, network television has made a bit of a comeback. The reason?

Content. Networks, because they remain the big dog on the block, are spending more on programming, and the viewers are starting to notice.

BIGresearch polled over 13,000 consumers about their media usage habits and discovered that young men are rapidly leaving TV in search

FIGURE 10.5 *Number of 18- to 34-Year-Old Men Who Use New Media in Their Leisure Time*

Activity	August 2002	March 2003	October 2003
Play video games	52.5%	55.6%	57.5%
Surf the Internet	68.3%	67.8%	72.0%
E-mail/Instant messaging	N/A	51.3%	55.5%

The sum of the percent totals may be greater than 100 percent because the respondents can select more than one answer.
Source: BIGresearch, 2003.

of other, more-interactive forms of entertainment, such as instant messaging and the Internet. (See Figure 10.5.) Fall television ratings show that viewing by the 18–34 group has declined by 7.7 percent. But Internet use, e-mailing, IM, and gaming have skyrocketed. The number of men in this age group who surf the Internet increased to 72 percent, up from 68.3 percent the prior year. Video game use increased 5 percent to 57.5 percent in the same period.

Men 18 to 34 reported spending 187.4 minutes daily using the Internet or e-mail, the most time spent with any medium. Still, these same respondents watched television 160.8 minutes on an average day.

THE MOST EFFECTIVE FORM OF MARKETING IS WORD OF MOUTH

Whatever is happening with electronic media continues to pale in the light of an even bigger fact—the most effective form of advertising is positive word of mouth. (See *Positively Outrageous Service,* Dearborn Trade, 2004.) As we mentioned earlier, our surveys show that the most influential medium is word of mouth (36.5 percent) and that 23 percent of the population are considered the go-to guys and gals when it comes to spreading the word. Find and cultivate your 20 percent and watch the effectiveness of your media multiply!

WHEN CUSTOMERS TALK

The grandkids are here. The Big Guy and the Princess are draped across big overstuffed chairs in the living room, each munching from a small bowl of grapes. The Big Guy likes the green ones, while the Princess likes the "pink ones." We know that because we listen to them. We also turn the chairs sideways, because the kids like to lay across them, using one arm of the chair for a pillow and the other as a place to rest their feet.

Did I hear you say, "You don't use a chair like that, do you?" You do if you're the Big Guy or if you just happen to be "the prettiest girl in the whole, wide world." You do if you're at Pops and Granny Buns's house.

We know what you like because we listen. If you are at Sporty's and you don't see your game on the television, we'll change the channel and tell you, "This is America! You're at Sporty's, and you can watch what you want!" Our regular customers aren't afraid to ask, because they know we'll listen. They tell us exactly what it takes to make them happy.

Your customers will talk to you, too. They'll tell you exactly what it takes to make them happy. (They told us and we're complete strangers!) Just imagine what you can learn once you gain a reputation for listening . . . when customers talk!

For more information, visit http://www.whencustomerstalk.com.

MONTHLY UPDATES FOR BUYERS OF THIS BOOK

Each month, BIGresearch surveys the largest continuous online consumer panel (8,000–10,000 people) to gauge their attitudes toward the economy, financial plans, product usage, and shopping behaviors for over 12 merchandise lines. The survey is called the Consumer Intentions and Actions survey (CIA for short), and it's the voice of the consumer for many of the top retailers in America.

Some of the most unique insights in the CIA come from the future purchase intentions of consumers. These planned expenditures serve as an early warning system for retailers and marketers of consumer products; that is, will consumer expenditures over the next 90 days be partly cloudy or sunny?

As an added bonus to each buyer of *When Customers Talk,* you are entitled to receive BIGresearch's exclusive video e-mail update of the CIA each month. The briefing will keep you updated on what customers are talking about and help you make valuable marketing decisions.

To register for your free subscription, visit our online subscription site at http://www.whencustomerstalk.com.

The stories and style of *When Customers Talk* come from the same mind that brought the world the management classic, *Positively Outrageous Service*. T. Scott Gross is a master at removing mystery, making complex ideas easy to understand and put to work. His stories about service techniques, customer foibles, and corporate missteps are revealing and memorable for the lessons they teach.

Scott has been working with clients to help them manage the service experience. Countless businesses, including Southwest Airlines, FedEx, McDonald's, Wal-Mart, and Sears, have asked Scott to motivate the troops at major sales meetings and conferences. He speaks from experience, having had hands-on experience as a franchisor and franchisee. Once again a restaurateur, Scott, with his wife and partner Melanie (Buns), consciously live their mission statement—Have fun and make the world a better place.

You can contact them at http://www.tscottgross.com or if you are in the neighborhood of Kerrville, Texas, stop and say hey at Sporty's, a Casual Café.

BIGresearch is a premiere online consumer intelligence company bringing new ideas for measuring and responding to the changing consumer marketplace. These BIG ideas, outside the old-fashioned research paradigm, deliver answers and solutions for creating winning marketing strategies and tactics that impact the top line, while dramatically decreasing the overall cost of research.

BIG's unique ability to gather large samples, apply computer-intensive statistical methods, and use unique proprietary software enables us to provide a new level of consumer insight and one of the highest levels of accuracy available within the industry.

We have a suite of intelligence products that enables management to chart a successful course through uncertain times by pinpointing where the consumer and marketplace are going, so you can quickly recognize and respond to change. Think of BIG as "radar for managers."

SYNDICATED RESEARCH

- BIGresearch's syndicated *Consumer Intentions and Actions (CIA)* survey monitors the pulse of over 8,000 consumers each month, delivering fresh, demand-based information on where the retail consumer is shopping and how their behavior is changing.
- The syndicated *Simultaneous Media Usage Survey (SIMM),* available for specific retailers or targeted consumer groups, provides a tool to understand the interrelationships of multiple media usage and how they impact the effectiveness and ROI of marketing expenditures.
- *The Retail Rating Report (RRR)* is a syndicated product that provides a monthly scorecard for the retail industry to determine who are the top performers from the consumer's point of view. Used as an "early warning system"to detect and monitor shifts in a retailer's customer base, it compares and analyzes the growth of consumer market share of retailers for key merchandise categories by gender, age, income, and geography.

CUSTOM SOLUTIONS

BIGresearch creates Proprietary Online Consumer Panels for our clients that have an ongoing need to gather intelligence and consumer insights. We do more research for less, while increasing the speed and turnaround of market studies.

KNOWLEDGE MINING

BIGresearch gives you the opportunity to license access to our massive database in order to discover relationships appropriate and unique to your business. Our large sample size and proprietary software dynamically weights and balances 14 age/sex cells and enables you to perform very granular analysis or even link with other databases.

BIG IDEA

More than ever, managers are under extreme pressure to deliver results, measure performance, and demonstrate return on investment. Our clients in retail, media, manufacturing, financial, and CPG industries are finding that market growth and leadership lie outside doing what others do, saying what others say, and offering what others offer. They are using BIGresearch to find ways to innovate. And that's one BIG idea! http://www.BIGresearch.com/talkhtm